Zany Wooden Toys RELOADED!

MORE Wild Projects from the Toy Inventor's Workshop

Bob Gilsdorf

FOX CHAPEL PUBLISHING

Dedication

This book is dedicated to my wonderful wife and best friend whose kindness, help, and wonderful smile made this all possible. The projects are dedicated to our five adventurous kids who have started inventing their own toys, to my Mom and Dad for always being creative, and to all the new inventors and toy builders who had fun making the zany projects in the first book.

Acknowledgments

Making toys is one thing. Making a book is something completely different and requires a great team to make it happen. I'd like to thank Peg Couch and Katie Weeber for figuring out how to make a book out of a few sketches and cryptic notes. I'd also like to thank Ayleen Stellhorn for putting the letters, words, and punctuation in the proper places. Additional thanks goes to Scott Kriner for photographing my work and to Jason Deller for a fantastic design. Finally, a special thanks to Jeremy for lending his drafting skill, Adam for his artwork, Sawyer for being a hand model, Noah for being the brave toy test pilot, and Ben for his solid encouragement. What a great team!

Don't shoot people or animals

There are some toys in this book that launch objects through the air or shoot objects across the ground. Be extremely careful not to aim at any people or animals. If you want to shoot at something, line up some action figures or cans and bottles. You could even create your own wooden target!

© 2013 by Bob Gilsdorf and Fox Chapel Publishing Company, Inc., East Petersburg, PA.

Zany Wooden Toys Reloaded! is an original work, first published in 2013 by Fox Chapel Publishing Company, Inc. The patterns contained herein are copyrighted by the author. Readers may make copies of these patterns for personal use. The patterns themselves, however, are not to be duplicated for resale or distribution under any circumstances. Any such copying is a violation of copyright law.

ISBN 978-1-56523-730-8

Library of Congress Cataloging-in-Publication Data

Gilsdorf, Bob, 1963-
  Zany wooden toys reloaded! : more wild projects from the toy inventor's workshop / Bob Gilsdorf.
    pages cm
  Includes index.
    Summary: "Your mission is to invent, build and control wild and wacky toys! Are you up for the challenge? This madcap follow-up to Zany Wooden Toys that Whiz, Spin, Pop, and Fly is sure to thrill the ten-year-old creator in your life. Zany Wooden Toys Reloaded! is packed with author Bob Gilsdorf's best and most creative projects. Disarm spy robots, launch flying discs, throw cards magically across the room--each of these imaginative woodworking projects ranks high on the fun scale! Inside you'll find 8 show-stopping creations that will delight kids and adults alike: -Magician's Envy Cardthrower -Boomerang Launcher -Bottle Cap Shooter -Pirate Coin Maker -Crayon Dispenser -Desktop Flicker-er -Knobby Knocker -Energy Orb Robot Battle -Gumball Smackdown "-- Provided by publisher.
    ISBN 978-1-56523-730-8 (pbk.)
  1. Wooden toy making. I. Title.
  TT174.5.W6G553 2013
  745.592--dc23
                          2012048665

To learn more about the other great books from Fox Chapel Publishing, or to find a retailer near you, call toll-free 800-457-9112 or visit us at *www.FoxChapelPublishing.com*.

Note to Authors: We are always looking for talented authors to write new books. Please send a brief letter describing your idea to Acquisition Editor, 1970 Broad Street, East Petersburg, PA 17520.

Printed in China
First printing

Introduction

I hope you're reading this book because you want to experience the thrill of the invention process, have a ball building an action toy, and discover how your contraption works and what games you can create. This is certainly what drove me to sketch out a bunch of crazy ideas, venture into the garage (my workshop), destroy it with sawdust and shavings, rack my brain wondering why such a great idea didn't work, and then do it all over again until, finally, *success*. My hope is that this book will hone your skills and give you some fresh ideas so you can start inventing right away. I can't wait to see what you create.

PHOTO BY DANI ST. ONGE

My love of building and inventing may have started with the first line I drew or the first nail I pounded into a board. As a kid, my favorite books featured awesome inventors like Captain Nemo, who made the spectacular submarine in Jules Verne's *20,000 Leagues Under the Sea*. My favorite movie was *Chitty Chitty Bang Bang* because the main character was a quirky inventor who had created a most fascinating breakfast-making machine and a flying car. These characters were my idols not only because they had great ideas, but because they could also figure out anything they needed.

My friend Scott and I were perhaps the weird kids on the block because we'd ride our bikes to the store, look at the toys, and then combine our money to buy nails. For my birthday during fifth grade, I simply told my parents, "I just want to build something." They surprised me with a steering wheel from a junkyard, a bunch of wood, a few bolts, a little rope, and four brand new wagon wheels. My mom and dad had put together everything needed for my first gravity-powered go-kart. Awesome! Needless to say, I was the envy of the neighborhood with my wooden hot rod. From that point on I was hooked on bringing ideas to life.

I found plenty of books and magazines to teach and inspire my young inventor's spirit. I bought plans from magazines like *Popular Mechanics* for the Bartlett Flying Saucer, a laser pistol, a rocket engine, a metal detector, and more. My success with these projects was, ummm, exactly 0%. (Thanks anyway, Mom, for driving me all over town in search of components that were as foreign to you as

Zany Wooden Toys Reloaded!

they were to me.) Those crazy dream projects were all way over my head, but each one was inspiring because someone had been able to dream the impossible and then figure out how to make it real. In between the science fiction projects, I succeeded at building things that were more at my skill level.

Making toys really kicked off when my wife Peggy and I started our family. My five little worker-men helped build things right from the beginning. We made cars for their teddy bears, golf clubs for the backyard, boats for sailing in the river, and anything else they could imagine. They were all crudely built and kid-decorated with crayons, markers, and paint, but each one was absolutely perfect in my children's eyes. As my kids grew, their skills improved and their ideas got bigger. They wanted toys that did something: action toys. We had a great time trying to figure out how to make and build them. The ones that worked were really fun, and I want to share them with anyone else who just wants to build something.

I thought back to all the books that I'd read and felt that something had been missing. All those books showed very precisely how to build each project. They never really admitted that there might have been mistakes along the way. As a kid I always thought that the invention process started with a supremely intelligent person who got a miraculously clear idea, drew up very detailed plans, built it perfectly, and yelled "Eureka!" when it worked exactly as expected. That's not how it happens.

The invention starts with a vague, fuzzy idea, and then there's a lot of experimenting trying to figure out what works, or, more realistically, what doesn't work. Sometimes projects go in radically different directions than the original idea. Sometimes ideas stall out and just need to sit for a long while. Having first-pass success is very rare—at least for me.

So this book is a little different. I show the original idea and some of the thought process used to start construction. I also unabashedly show a few of the mistakes I made and challenges I encountered. Each challenge makes the final success even more rewarding. Learn from the mistakes and take the challenges head on. The answer will eventually come, and when it does, yelling "Eureka!" sure feels good. Go start building and creating your own amazing toys.

Bob

I'd love to see what you've made, how you decorated it, and how you modified it to make it even better. Drop me an email and photo at *ideas@thetoyinventorsworkshop.com*.

Contents

Magician's Envy Card Thrower
page 34

Desktop Flicker-er
page 80

Boomerang Launcher
page 47

Pirate Coin Maker
page 65

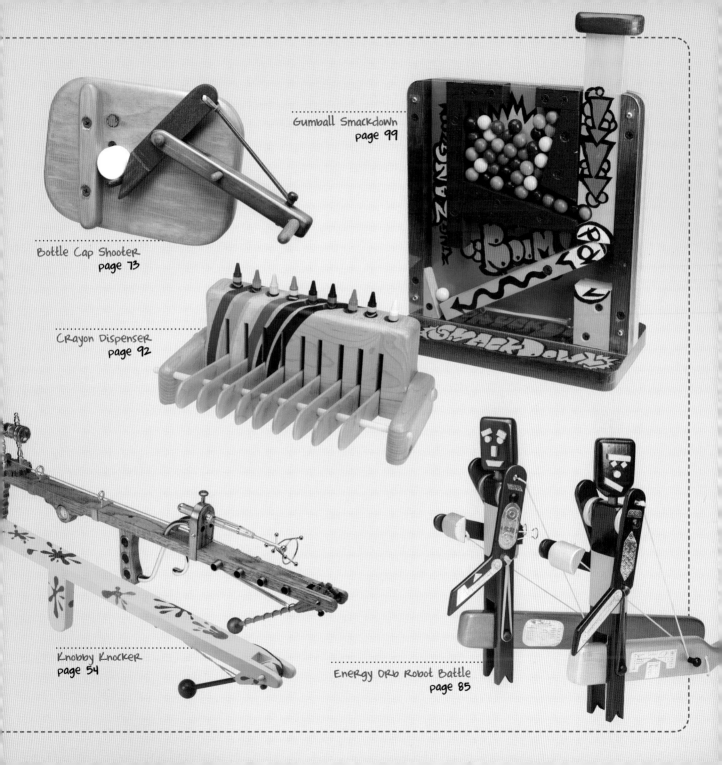

Gumball Smackdown
page 99

Bottle Cap Shooter
page 73

Crayon Dispenser
page 92

Knobby Knocker
page 54

Energy Orb Robot Battle
page 85

Woodworking Basics

The toys in this book are primarily made out of wood. Why wood? The main reason is that wood is an ideal material for inventors. It's easy to find, easy to work with, fairly strong, and inexpensive. You can cut it, shape it, connect it, and decorate it with basic tools. You can also put in a little more time sanding and finishing the project and end up with a beautiful work of art.

The woodworking instructions in this book are geared toward providing the basics so that your ideas can take shape. There are many great books on woodworking that show the finer points of choosing wood, using tools, making precise joints, and creating fine finishes. For now, we're interested in capturing the prototype in wood just to see if it works. If we like it, then we'll make another one and take more time to make it a work of art.

SELECTING WOOD

Wood is a wonderful building material because it is strong, easy to work with, and easy to find. You need to know just a little about wood so you can walk into a hardware store with confidence and quickly get all the supplies you need to start work on your inventions.

Boards

All of the toys in this book were originally made with basic, construction-grade pine boards or plywood. This wood is readily available at hardware stores and lumberyards and comes in standard sizes. Make your first toys with inexpensive but good wood. You can always experiment with more interesting varieties later.

Sizes

Wood is sold in standard dimensions. The toys in this book were designed around these standard dimensions whenever possible to avoid having to make extra cuts. However, these dimensions can be a little deceiving when you're buying wood.

The wood is sold by the dimensions from which it was originally cut from the tree, such as 2" (51mm) thick by 4" (102mm) wide by so many feet long. The large saw used to make these cuts leaves a very rough, splintery surface on the boards. Luckily, the sawmill is kind enough to plane the boards smooth so woodworkers don't spend too much time removing splinters. The drawback is that the 2" x 4" (51 x 102mm) board is now only 1½" x 3½" (38 x 89mm). The sawmill took off ¼" (6mm) on each side. However, the board is still called a "two by four." For thinner boards, the sawmill takes off less. So, for example, a 1" x 6" (25 x 152mm) board ends up being ¾" x 5½" (19 x 140mm).

What this really means is that the more you work with wood, the better you become with fractions. The supply lists in this book call out the actual dimensions.

Construction-grade pine is a good choice for the projects in this book.

How to choose good wood

Choosing good wood is not difficult, but there are a few things you'll want to watch for.

- **Warp:** Make sure the board lies flat on the floor and doesn't bend up or bend sideways. Look down the length of the board to ensure that it is straight.

- **Cracks:** Look at the ends of the boards to see if there are cracks. Cracks will be weak spots in your project.

- **Knots:** Knots are the dark circles that you see on most boards. They look nice, but they are very, very hard. Thus, they are difficult to nail, drill, and saw. Choose wood with few knots, and lay out your patterns to avoid them.

- **Other damage:** Boards can often have rough areas, scratches, or paint on them. You won't want to use that wood for your projects, so try to find boards that are as clean as possible.

Damaged and knotty boards will make construction difficult.

NOMINAL BOARD SIZE VS. ACTUAL SIZE

Board Size	Actual Size	Lingo
1" x 2" (25 x 51mm)	¾" x 1½" (19 x 38mm)	one by two
1" x 4" (25 x 102mm)	¾" x 3½" (19 x 89mm)	one by four
1" x 6" (25 x 152mm)	¾" x 5½" (19 x 140mm)	one by six
1" x 8" (25 x 203mm)	¾" x 7½" (19 x 191mm)	one by eight
1" x 12" (25 x 305mm)	¾" x 11" (19 x 279mm)	one by twelve
2" x 4" (51 x 102mm)	1½" x 3½" (38 x 89mm)	two by four
2" x 6" (51 x 152mm)	1½" x 5½" (38 x 140mm)	two by six

Wood grain

The grain of the wood is the pattern of lines that you see in it. The grain lines run up and down the trunk of the tree and up and down the length of a pine board. The grain is important for two reasons: 1) looks and 2) strength. For now, we care only about strength.

Boards are stronger in the direction of the grain and weaker across the grain. To demonstrate this, cut about ¼" (6mm) off the end of a 1 x 4 board. Cut a similar size piece along the length of the board. Now, try to break the pieces. The board with end grain will snap very easily. The section cut with the long grain will be very difficult to break. This is important when laying out toys. Avoid using end grain on small pieces. When this is unavoidable, lay out the piece at a 45° angle to the grain.

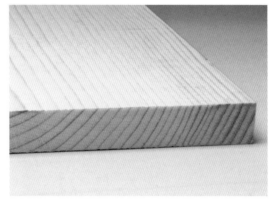

End grain can be seen on the end of a board.

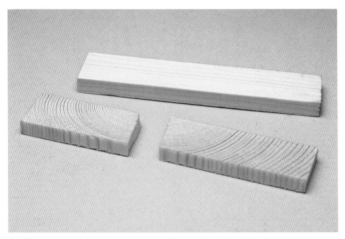

End-grain pieces break easily, but the section cut with the grain is strong.

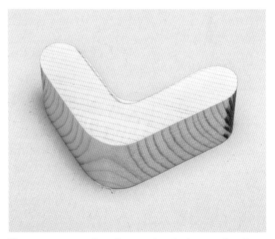

If you must cut a piece from end grain, lay out the piece at a 45° angle to the grain.

Plywood

Plywood is made by gluing thin layers of wood together. Each layer is placed with the grain perpendicular to the layer below. This creates a very strong, flat board. This strength is important for thin pieces (⅛" [3mm] and ¼" [6mm] thick) and for small pieces. Plywood comes in different quality grades, depending on the type of wood used, how smooth the surface is, and the type of glue used. Inexpensive plywood will work just fine for the projects in this book.

Dowels

Dowels are great! They are truly indispensable. They serve as axles, hinge pins, ramrods, and anchors for rubber bands. Dowels come in a variety of diameters and lengths. The projects in this book use dowels with ¼" (6mm), ⅜" (10mm), ½" (13mm), and 1" (25mm) diameters. The diameters of dowels can be fairly unpredictable. Due to machining, they are not always perfectly round, and some will fit loosely in the hole while others will be too tight. For loose dowels, just wrap the dowel with a piece of tape or add a splinter of wood into the hole. For tight dowels, sanding will work.

Plywood is made by gluing many layers of wood together, with each layer perpendicular to those on both sides of it.

Dowels are available in a variety of diameters.

MAKING CUTS

Few projects can be made with full-length boards. Thus, you're going to have to learn how to cut boards down to size and how to shape them the way you want.

Straight cuts

If you need to cut a straight line, you'll want to use a handsaw. Handsaws are specifically designed for making straight cuts. A handsaw blade is wide and stiff, which makes it very easy to follow a straight line.

There are many types of handsaws in different sizes. For the projects in this book, you only need to be concerned about two things: 1) how many teeth per inch on the blade and 2) the length of the blade. The more teeth per inch a saw has, the cleaner the cut will be. A saw with 7 to 10 teeth per inch (TPI) will work fine. Saws come in sizes of about 12" (305mm), 15" (381mm), 20" (508mm), and 26" (660mm). Because the projects in this book are small, a 12" (305mm) or 15" (381mm) saw will be fine. Larger saws may be awkward to use on small pieces.

Miter Saw and Miter Box

A miter saw and miter box work together to help improve the accuracy of your straight cuts. The miter box acts as a guide for the miter saw so you don't have to worry about keeping the blade straight. The simplest miter boxes are made out of plastic or wood. There are grooves in the miter box to hold the saw at set angles of 90°, 45°, and other angles. Follow the same steps as you would for using a handsaw. Remember to clamp your wood in the miter box, because small pieces are difficult to hold steady.

Handsaws come in a variety of saw tooth sizes and teeth per inch.

HOW TO MAKE A STRAIGHT CUT

1 Mark your cutline on the top and side of the board to ensure the cut starts out at the correct angle. You will be cutting right next to the lines you marked. If you were to cut directly on the lines, your piece would end up slightly smaller than you intended due to the wood removed by the saw (also known as the saw kerf). I always put a small "X" on the side of the line that will be the waste, as a reminder of where to place the saw.

2 Clamp the wood so that the cutline is vertical. Make sure there's enough room for the saw. It is a good idea to put scrap wood between the clamp and the project piece to prevent any squashing.

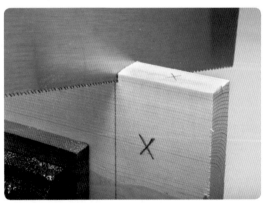

3 Start the cut by placing the back of the blade (i.e., the part nearest the handle) next to the pencil line on the corner farthest from your hand. Tilt the saw slightly downward. Your arm should line up with the line on the wood. Slowly pull back the saw. This will start the cut at the corner and leave a small groove. Repeat this several times to ensure that the saw is following your marks.

4 After a few backstrokes, start sawing with a slow back-and-forth motion. Make long, even strokes. Finish the cut by slowing down and using less downward pressure when you have about ¼" (6mm) left to go. Support the waste portion of the board with your free hand to prevent it from breaking loose and tearing out a splinter.

Cutting with a coping saw

Use a coping saw for making curved cuts. It has a narrow, flexible blade that can change direction easily. The narrower the blade is, the tighter the curve it can cut. Coping saws cut on the pull stroke to prevent the blade from bending or buckling. Each end of the blade is connected to a pin that can rotate in the frame. This gives you much more freedom when cutting larger pieces. Just remember that the pins should always point in the same direction.

You can remove or replace the blade in a coping saw by turning the handle counterclockwise with respect to the frame. This will loosen the blade so that you can remove one or both ends.

Coping saws are used to cut curved lines.

HOW TO MAKE A CURVED CUT

1 Clamp your marked work piece vertically in a vise. Thin pieces tend to vibrate, so clamp as near to the cut as possible.

2 Start the cut by laying the blade flat against the cutline. Use several backstrokes to start the cut.

3 Control the cut by placing your index finger on the coping saw's frame. Keep the blade perpendicular to the face of the wood so that the saw pattern on the back is the same as on the front. Rotate the frame as needed to finish the cut.

4 Rotate the blade to prevent the frame from hitting the wood when making deep cuts.

HOW TO MAKE A SQUARE CUT

Use the coping saw to remove square pieces of wood. This requires four different cuts.

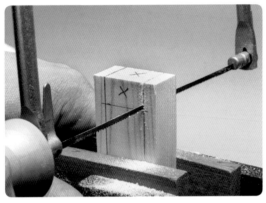

1 Cut down the right side.

2 Cut down the left side.

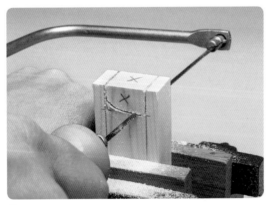

3 Back the saw a short distance out of the second cut, and create a curved cut that meets up with the bottom of the first cut.

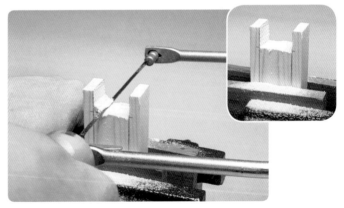

4 Starting at the bottom of the first cut, saw horizontally back to the bottom of the second cut.

Rabbets

"Rabbet" is just woodworking language for a channel or groove that is cut in the end of a board. It is made with two straight cuts. One cut is across the grain, and the other is on the end grain.

HOW TO MAKE A RABBET

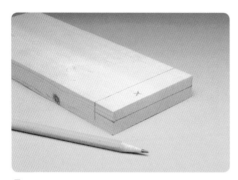

1 Mark the width and depth of the rabbet on the top, end, and sides of the board. There will be six lines.

2 Clamp the board to a horizontal surface. Use your handsaw to cut down across the grain to the first mark. Make sure the saw hits the marks on the front and back edges.

3 Reclamp your board so that the end grain is facing upward. Make the second cut on the end grain to complete the rabbet. The channel can be cleaned up with a chisel if need be.

DRILLING HOLES

Round holes are a toymaker's friend. They form an important part of axles, hinges, and latches. The best part about holes is that they are very easy to make.

Drills

Hand drills—the human-powered ones—are fun to use, and there's a great sense of accomplishment with each hole made. However, I highly recommend using a very basic corded or cordless power drill. I find that I'm much more accurate when I'm free to concentrate on aligning the bit straight up and down.

The basic power drill has two parts of interest: 1) the trigger and 2) the chuck. Power drills have a pistol-style handle that allows you to drill holes with one hand. Your index finger activates the trigger—a gentle squeeze will start the drill. The chuck holds the different bits used for making holes. Get a drill with a chuck that can open up to ⅜" (10mm).

Hand drills are powered by muscle.

Cordless power drills allow you to focus on drilling a straight hole.

Drill bits

There are many different kinds of bits, and almost all sizes are available. Buy a set of 15 to 20 drill bits ranging from ⅛" (4mm) to ½" (13mm). The larger bits should have shanks no larger than ⅜" (10mm) to fit into your chuck.

Twist bits: Their spiral, or twisted, shape allows these bits to easily cut through wood, plastic, and metal. Twist drill bits are the most basic type of bit.

Brad tip bits: Also known as dowel bits, brad tip bits have a sharp point that prevents the bit from wandering when drilling into grainy or curved surfaces.

Forstner bits: These bits excel at cutting clean holes and are good for holes that enter the wood at an angle.

Spade bits: Chisel bits come in larger diameters but tend to tear the wood when exiting.

Hole-cutting bits: These are useful for very large holes.

Countersink bits: A countersink bit is also good to have. It creates a conical-shaped depression around an already drilled hole. This is needed to recess screw heads below the surface of the wood. A countersink bit is used just like a regular drill bit, but you apply just enough pressure to make an indentation the size of the screw you are using.

Helpful Hints for Drilling

Put a piece of masking tape on the drill when you need to drill holes to a certain depth.

Prevent splintering around the exit hole of your work piece by drilling into a piece of scrap wood. With practice, you'll be able to feel when you've drilled through the top piece.

Make the exit hole cleaner by drilling the hole just deep enough for the center of the bit to poke through the other side. Flip the board over, and start drilling where the bit poked through.

There are many types of drill bits, including Forstner (left), brad tip (middle left), twist (middle), countersink (bottom), hole-cutting (right top), and chisel (right).

HOW TO DRILL A HOLE

1 Mark the location for the hole with an awl. This small indentation will prevent the bit from wandering away from the hole.

2 Clamp the wood in a vise so that the hole can be drilled with the bit straight up and down.

3 Align the bit so it is perpendicular to the work surface. The bit should be resting on the mark from the awl.

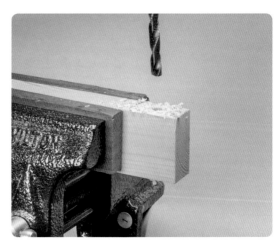

4 Squeeze the trigger to start drilling. Apply minimal downward force—the weight of the drill should be enough. Clear the sawdust out of the hole every inch or so by backing the drill bit almost completely out of the hole with the drill still running. This will prevent sawdust from clogging the spirals in the drill bit.

5 When your hole is complete, remove the drill while it is still spinning.

Zany Wooden Toys Reloaded!

CONNECTING WOOD

You will often be faced with the question of how to connect one piece of wood to another. The three basic methods are nailing, screwing, and gluing. (I put gluing last because when you're inventing something, you don't want to disrupt your creativity and excitement by having to wait for glue to dry.) Knowing the advantages and disadvantages of each method will help you choose what's right for your project.

Nailing

Nails are the most common way of connecting one piece of wood to another. This method of connecting relies on the friction between the wood and the nail to hold the pieces together. Nails make a quick and fairly sturdy connection. However, while they are very strong when the force on them is sideways to the nail, they are not as strong when the force is attempting to pull the nail out.

Box nails have large heads to hold the boards together. Finishing nails have small heads that are pushed below the wood surface using a nail set for a more attractive finish (if you think nail heads are ugly).

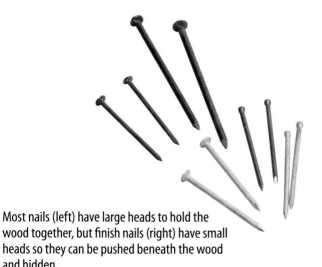

Most nails (left) have large heads to hold the wood together, but finish nails (right) have small heads so they can be pushed beneath the wood and hidden.

ADVANTAGES AND DISADVANTAGES OF NAILS

Advantages	Disadvantages
Fast to use	Wood can split due to the sideways force of the nail
Reasonably strong connection	May not be strong enough; especially weak in end grain
Not permanent	Can be difficult to remove
	Pounding on your project can loosen other pieces

NAIL PROBLEMS AND SOLUTIONS

Problem	Solution
Wood splits	The nail was too close to the edge. Use the claw to pull the nail out and move it farther from the edge.
Nail bends	Most likely, the hammer is hitting the nail at an angle. Make sure the handle of the hammer is parallel to the top piece.
Nail still bends	You may be hitting a knot in the wood. Move to a new location.
Nail pokes through the second piece of wood	The nail was started crooked. Turn the project upside down, and pound the tip of the nail back into the wood so you can grab the nail head with the claw. Try again using a different hole.
Your thumb hurts	If the nails are small, you might want to hold them with needle-nose pliers.

HOW TO NAIL

1 Choose the correct size hammer. For small projects, choose a smaller hammer (5 to 10 ounces).

2 Choose the appropriate size nail. As a rule of thumb, the nail should go into the second board about twice the thickness of the first board. For example, if you're nailing through a ¼" (6mm) board, the nail should be about ¾" (19mm) long.

3 Determine where to place each nail, and make a small mark. Don't place nails too close to the edge of a board, because the wood might split. You need to pound in at least two nails to keep the top piece from rotating. Separate the nails by about twice their length.

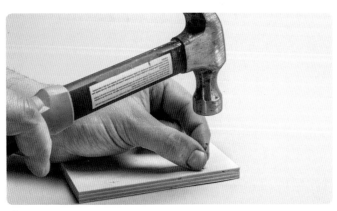

4 Start each nail in the top piece by holding it between your thumb and index finger and tapping it with the hammer. The nail should be straight up-and-down above the mark. The face of the hammer should be perpendicular to the nail. Pound in the nails just deep enough so they don't fall over.

5 Align the top piece and the bottom piece, and finish pounding in all the nails.

Zany Wooden Toys Reloaded!

Screwing

Screws take a little more time than nails, but are often necessary when you want extra strength. Screws excel at pulling two pieces of wood together. The threads of the screw cut into the wood and provide extra grip—it is nearly impossible to pull out a screw. Making a hole for a typical flathead wood screw requires three different bits: one for the pilot hole, one for the clearance hole, and a countersink bit.

There are many types of screws, but for inventors, nothing beats a coarse-threaded drywall screw for ease of use and speed. If you're using short screws in softwood, such as pine, you can take a shortcut and skip all the drilling. Just make sure you hold the boards tightly together while putting in the screws. Most of the time, however, it is worth the effort to drill a clearance hole. A pilot hole may not be necessary all the time, but it will prevent the wood from splitting and make it easier to insert the screw. Drywall screws usually do a good job of countersinking themselves. If the screw head is on the bottom of your project, however, you'll want to countersink the hole to prevent the screw head from scratching any surfaces.

Screws are a secure method for attaching pieces of wood.

ADVANTAGES AND DISADVANTAGES OF SCREWS	
Advantages	**Disadvantages**
Very strong	Drill, drill bit, and screwdriver are needed
Project can be disassembled	Slower than nailing
Pulls wood together	May need to drill three holes
No pounding on your project	

SCREW PROBLEMS AND SOLUTIONS	
Problem	**Solution**
You've been turning for hours, and it's not going in	All screws go in clockwise. The saying is "Lefty loosey, righty tighty."
It's very hard to turn	You may have made the pilot hole too small. Before you get out the drill, try rubbing a little bar soap on the screw and putting the screw in again.
The screw keeps turning	The pilot hole is too wide, so the threads don't have enough wood to grab. Put a splinter of wood about the size of a wooden match in the hole, and try putting the screw in again.

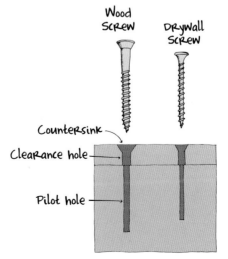

To insert a screw, you usually need to drill a pilot hole, a clearance hole, and a countersink.

HOW TO INSERT A SCREW

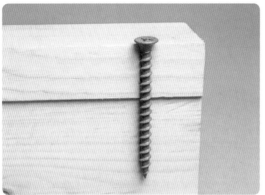

1 Choose the correct size screw. The rule of thumb for a nail also applies for a screw: It should go into the second board about twice the thickness of the first board. That's one-third in the top board and two-thirds in the bottom board.

2 Align the pieces, and drill the pilot hole. To determine the size of the pilot hole, hold a small drill bit in front of the screw. The drill bit should cover only the solid metal portion between the threads. The pilot hole also should be slightly shorter than the screw. You can mark this depth on the drill bit using a piece of tape.

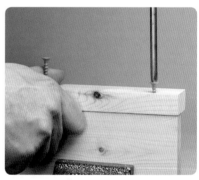

3 Drill the clearance hole through the top piece. The clearance hole is the width of the body of the screw. The screw should be able to pass through this hole without having to be turned. To determine the size of the clearance hole, hold a bit in front of the screw. This time, the drill bit should just cover the threads.

4 Drill the countersink hole. This hole is made so the head of the screw is below the level of the wood. Use a countersink bit, and apply just enough pressure to make a small indentation.

5 Use a Phillips (cross) or standard (flat) screwdriver to insert the screw. Screw it in until the boards are held together tightly.

Zany Wooden Toys Reloaded!

Gluing

Argh! I hate glue because it is so slooow. However, it does work well for holding wood together, and there are times when only glue will work. There are many different types of glue, including white glue, yellow glue, hot glue, and epoxy. White glue is what you typically buy for the first day of school. It works great on wood. If you go to a hardware store, buy yellow glue—the fancy name is aliphatic resin glue. It dries a little quicker than white glue. Both wash up with water, which is nice. Don't mess with other glues until your invention calls out for a superstrong, waterproof joint.

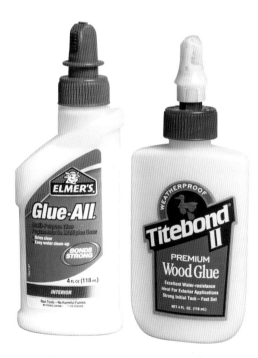

Glue is a secure fastener, but it often takes a long time to dry.

ADVANTAGES AND DISADVANTAGES OF GLUE	
Advantages	**Disadvantages**
Very strong connection	Slow
Can be used on very small pieces	Cannot be disassembled
Gives you time to clean up the shop	Requires clamping

GLUE PROBLEMS AND SOLUTIONS	
Problem	**Solution**
You don't have clamps	Try using rubber bands or putting weight, such as books or tools, on the pieces.
The glue dried, and the boards are in the wrong position	Start over.
You got bored waiting for the glue to dry and invented something else	Way to go!

HOW TO GLUE

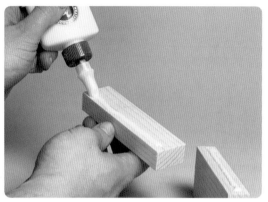

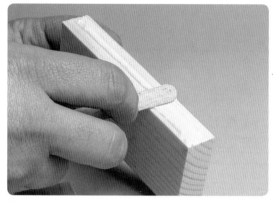

1 Make sure that the two surfaces to be glued are clean and free of oil, dirt, sawdust, or other stuff. Apply a small amount of glue to both surfaces.

2 Spread out the glue so it completely covers the surface. I like to use my finger, but you can also use a brush or a craft stick.

3 Align the pieces, and then hold them together using clamps. Apply just enough force to squeeze glue out on all sides. Fine woodworkers remove the extra glue after it has dried so that it doesn't interfere with the finish. Inventors wipe it up immediately because big blobs of glue take forever to dry.

DECORATING AND FINISHING

Decorating a project can be just as much fun as building it and playing with it. Decorating allows you to make your toy unique, whimsical, and interesting. You can put a little of your own personality and attitude into the toy. Don't underestimate the power of decorating to bring just as many smiles as the toy itself.

So now for the last crazy woodworking word: finish. A finish is a protective coating put on the wood to help preserve it and to bring out the beauty of the wood. There are many different types of finishes, and finishing a project can be very quick or can take a few days. Knowing the basics will help you choose the finish that's right for your project. When you finish finishing your project, you are truly finished.

Decorating and finishing are absolutely not necessary. I have yet to meet a kid who wants to wait around for paint or varnish to dry on a toy he or she just made.

Painting

Acrylic paints from a hobby store or an art store work very well on wood and come in an almost infinite variety of colors. These paints dry quickly and conveniently clean up with soap and water. A basic set of red, blue, and yellow will get you started. I also like to get orange, purple, and green so I don't have to mix those colors. These paints can be watered down so that they act more like stain and show the wood grain. Either way, you'll have a very colorful and fun project.

Acrylic paints and stains are great for decorating your project.

Kid-Friendly Decorating

If you're making toys with a little kid, let him or her do the decorating. Crayons, markers, and colored pencils work great on bare wood. These have an added benefit in that they will not interfere with moving parts.

WOODWORKING BASICS

HOW TO PAINT

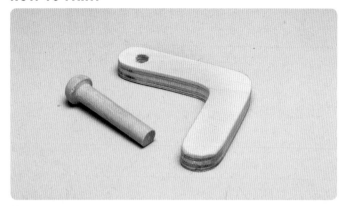

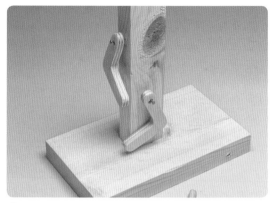

1 Disassemble the project if there are moving parts. Paint can act like glue and make moving parts stick. It is wise to paint the pieces separately.

2 Make a stand or lay out scrap wood to hold your project while it dries.

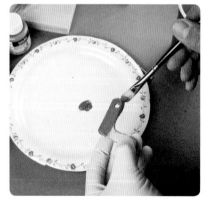

3 Get a glass of water for cleaning your brush and a few paper towels for drying it off. Then, squeeze a small amount of paint onto a paper plate.

4 Apply the first color by brushing on the paint in the direction of the grain. Let this layer dry before applying the next color to prevent mixing of colors.

5 Rinse your brush in the water until it leaves no color on the paper towel when you dry it. Add the next color. Don't forget to clean the brush in warm, soapy water when you're done painting. Work the bristles sideways to remove the paint; don't mash the bristles up and down. Lay the paintbrush on its side to dry.

Finishing

There are many different types of finishes available, including oils, varnishes, shellacs, and lacquers. The two easiest finishes to use are mineral oil and water-based finish. Mineral oil is applied by using a cloth to rub it on the wood. This is a nontoxic finish, so it's safe for young kids. Water-based finish provides a warm, clear finish that brings out the natural beauty of the wood. It is applied just like paint. Whichever water-based finish you choose, be mindful of potential health hazards with fumes or with the finish itself. Nontoxic paints and finishes, such as salad bowl finishes, can be found at specialty woodworking stores. Follow the directions on the product you choose, and you'll have a beautiful and safe toy.

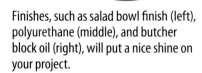

Finishes, such as salad bowl finish (left), polyurethane (middle), and butcher block oil (right), will put a nice shine on your project.

HOW TO USE A WATER-BASED FINISH

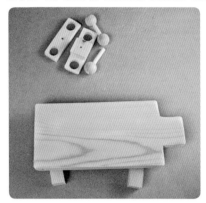

1 Disassemble the project if there are moving parts. Finish can act like glue and make moving parts stick. Lay out scraps of wood to hold your project while it dries.

2 Open the finish, and stir it with a paint stick. Do not shake the finish, because this will create bubbles and leave your finish bumpy.

3 Apply a layer of finish by brushing it on in the direction of the grain. Be careful to watch for drips at the edges.

4 Use very fine 000 or 0000 steel wool to rub down and smooth out the first layer of finish after it has thoroughly dried. Repeat Steps 2 and 3 for the second coat of finish. NOTE: See page 28, Step 5 for instructions on how to clean your brush when you are done.

Zany Wooden Toys Reloaded!

TOY-MAKING BASICS

You never know when an idea is going to pop into your head, so you should always be ready with a few supplies and basic toy-making know-how.

Always have some basic toy-making supplies on hand just in case you get a sudden bright idea.

Toy-making supplies

Basic toy-making supplies can be found at many hobby stores and woodworking supply stores. Here is what I always try to keep on hand:

- 1" (25mm) and 2" (51mm) wooden wheels with ¼" (6mm) holes
- ¾" (19mm) and 1" (25mm) wooden balls (with and without holes)
- ¼" (6mm) pegs
- ¼" (6mm) dowel caps
- Craft sticks (narrow and wide)
- Hook screws
- Eye screws
- Variety of nails
- Variety of screws
- Variety of rubber bands
- Clothespins
- Wood glue
- Duct tape
- Nylon string
- Cotton string

Zany Wooden Toys Reloaded!

Lubricating Wood

Usually, when you are making action toys out of wood, there will be places where one piece of wood rubs against another. This is often the case with latches, axles, gears, levers, and similar parts. Too much friction between the pieces can make the toy difficult or impossible to play with.

The first way to reduce friction is to make sure you sand both pieces smooth. If there's still too much friction, you'll need to add a lubricant.

Do not use oil! The wood will absorb the oil, swell, and make matters worse. Instead, try graphite or powdered Teflon. The quickest source for graphite is the end of your pencil. Just rub a little on the two surfaces, and everything should start moving again.

You can also buy tubes or bottles of powdered graphite and Teflon.

Graphite and other powdered lubricants are available commercially.

The easiest way to lubricate a moving part on a toy is to rub a pencil tip on both surfaces.

Working with Kids

Young kids love to be involved with projects, and they'll be even more eager to help out with a toy-making project. Building toys with your little ones is a great opportunity to teach, talk, laugh, and have fun together, but you'll need to combine simple directions with lots of patience. Here are some easy toy-making steps that are great for kids. As always, direct supervision is recommended.

- Carrying wood
- Marking and measuring
- Cutting with handsaws (with direct supervision)
- Clamping: Holding the clamp or twisting the handle
- Nailing: Have a helper hold the nail with needle-nose pliers to avoid bruised fingers
- Pounding in pegs
- Inserting screws
- Squeezing and spreading glue
- Inserting rubber bands
- Sanding
- Decorating with crayons, markers, and colored pencils

Time-saving tips

A key component to inventing toys is speed. Whether you're building with a kid or trying to capture your own idea, time is of the essence. Here are some tips on saving time.

1. Try to design toys that do not require gluing. Always consider nails, screws, and snug-fitting pegs before deciding to use glue.

2. Don't measure everything. Very few dimensions are critical. Most dimensions can just be eyeballed or estimated. For example, you can easily guess where the middle of a board is.

3. Most cuts don't have to be perfectly square. So rather than measuring a length and then using a square to lay out a perfectly straight, 90° line, just free-hand cut the board based on your one little pencil mark.

4. Drill all holes first. Review all of the holes needed so you don't have to keep changing bits.

5. Take advantage of the set dimensions of common lumber. For example, say you want to draw a line down the middle of a 1" (25mm) x 2" (51mm) board. You remember that the board is actually ¾" (19mm) x 1½" (38mm). The center of the 1 x 2 is ¾" (19mm). Thus, you can mark the center of the board by just using the ¾" (19mm) width of another board.

6. Find the center of a board by drawing straight lines from each corner to the opposite corner. Where the two lines cross is dead-center.

Safety

- Always wear eye protection when using cutting tools.

- Always wear ear protection when using power tools.

- Keep your fingers away from drills, blades, and other cutting edges.

- Clamp small pieces and spheres. Don't try to hold them in your hands when cutting or sawing.

- Use good ventilation when finishing your projects.

- Take good care of your tools so they'll work properly.

- Keep your work area clean.

- Don't rush.

- Keep toys with small pieces away from small children.

- If you make a toy that launches, shoots, pushes, flips, or somehow moves, make sure no one, including yourself, is in the way.

Projects

Now that you know the basics of working with the tools and supplies you'll need to make these projects, it's time for you to get busy creating! This section contains nine delightful and amusing projects that are sure to get your wheels turning. The first project is a step-by-step tutorial that takes you through each step of the process for making a magical card-throwing device. The remaining projects let you do some experimentation yourself, but don't worry, there are still plenty of helpful hints and engineering advice to steer you in the right direction. And remember, you can always adapt these projects to make them do something completely new. Use your imagination and expect some amazing results!

Magician's Envy
CARD THROWER
STEP-BY-STEP

With just a rubber band, a paper clip, and a little woodworking skill you'll be flinging cards across the yard in no time. This toy is very easy to make and the results are amazing. You'll be surprised how far and fast a card can travel. There's a little engineering to do as you figure out where to position the card and how much pinching force the paper clip needs, but that's part of the fun and learning.

Magicians can perform an amazing trick — throwing cards a very long distance.

There's no magic involved, just a strong wrist and lots of practice. I bet we can invent something that will also throw cards magically across the room.

MATERIALS

- ☑ ¾" x 2" x 15" (19 x 51 x 381mm) pine board for the handle
- ☑ ¾" x ¾" x 12" (19 x 19 x 305mm) pine board for the arm
- ☑ ½" (13mm) dowel, 3" (76mm) long for the arm stops
- ☑ 1" (25mm) peg or ¼" (6mm)-diameter dowel, 1¼" (32mm) long for the rubber band anchor
- ☑ 1¼" (32mm) coarse-thread drywall screw
- ☑ 1½" (38mm)- to 2" (51mm)-long paper clip
- ☑ #6 x ½" (13mm) pan head screw
- ☑ #6 washer
- ☑ 6" x ¼" (6mm) rubber band, or two #64, 3½" x ¼" (89 x 6mm) rubber bands connected together
- ☑ Two ¾" (19mm) brad nails
- ☑ Playing cards—fairly new

TOOLS

- ☑ Coping saw
- ☑ Vise
- ☑ Ruler or tape measure
- ☑ Pencil
- ☑ Square
- ☑ Hammer
- ☑ Drill
- ☑ ³⁄₁₆" (5mm), ⁷⁄₃₂" (5.5mm), and ½" (13mm) drill bits
- ☑ Screw drivers (Phillips and flat head)
- ☑ Awl, or nail, to mark screw locations
- ☑ Small piece of wire to thread the rubber band

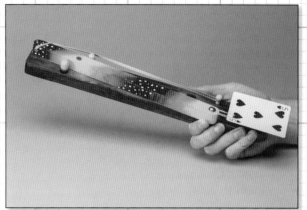

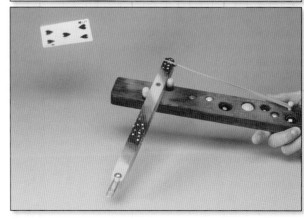

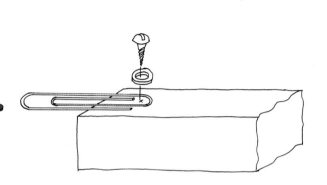

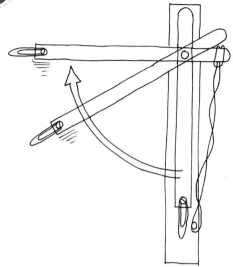

Holding the card: The magician pinches the card between his index finger and middle finger. A paper clip seems like the perfect pincher because that's what it was designed to do. A 1½" (38mm)- to 2" (51mm)-long paper clip should work. Hold it in place with a washer and a pan head screw.

Throwing the card: The magician snaps his wrist a little to spin the card and give it some forward motion. We'll do this by mounting the paper clip at the end of a wooden arm that pivots on a screw. This arm will be powered by a rubber band.

I know there's magic in my workshop because every time I set my screwdriver down it disappears!

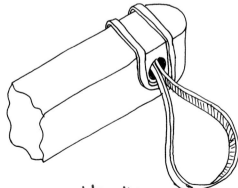

Connect the rubber band like this.

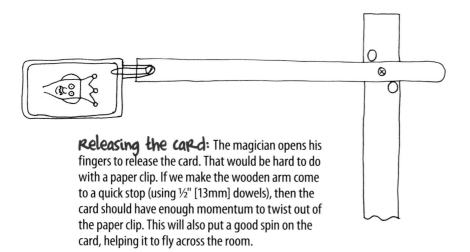

Releasing the card: The magician opens his fingers to release the card. That would be hard to do with a paper clip. If we make the wooden arm come to a quick stop (using ½" [13mm] dowels), then the card should have enough momentum to twist out of the paper clip. This will also put a good spin on the card, helping it to fly across the room.

Choose finger to release pivot arm.

What happens if you put in 2 or 3 cards?

Magician's Envy Card Thrower

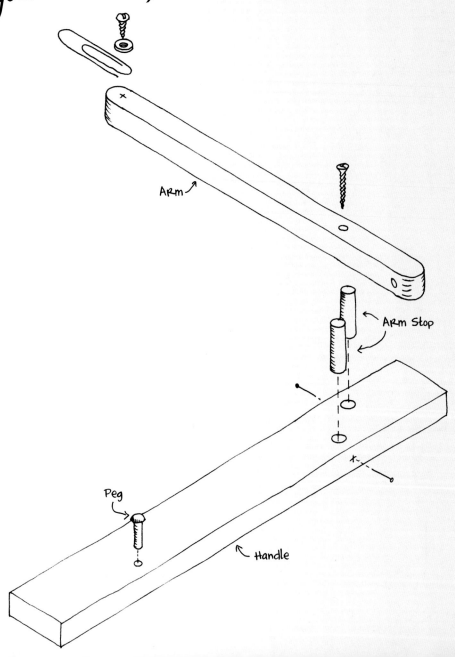

Arm

Arm Stop

Peg

Handle

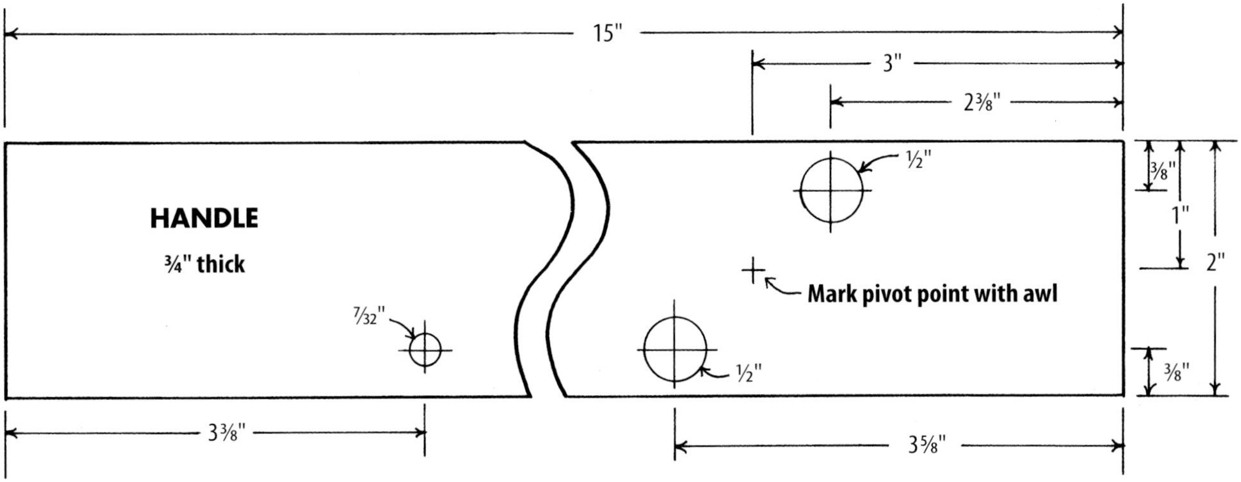
15"
3"
2⅜"
½"
HANDLE
¾" thick
Mark pivot point with awl
7/32"
½"
⅜"
1"
2"
⅜"
3⅜"
3⅝"

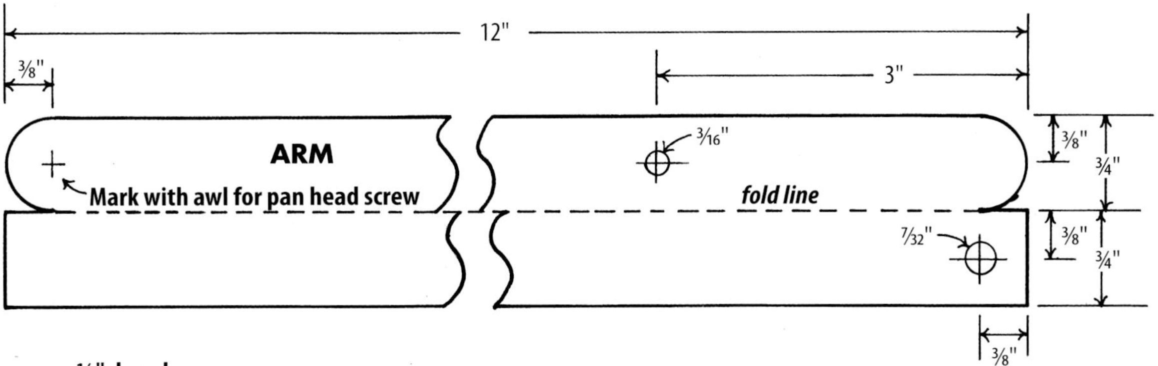
12"
⅜"
3"
ARM
3/16"
Mark with awl for pan head screw
fold line
7/32"
⅜"
¾"
⅜"
¾"
⅜"

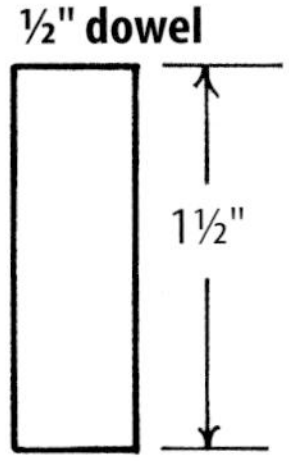
½" dowel
1½"

ARM STOP
Make 2

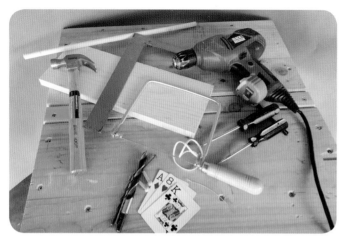

Cutting the handle and arm.

The handle and arm can be cut from a wider piece of ¾" (19mm)-thick wood. Just mark the 2" (51mm) or ¾" (19mm) width, mount the wood in a vise, and saw down the line. You may have to rotate the blade on your coping saw to make the cut.

1 Gather the supplies. Collect all of the supplies on the Materials & Tools list. If you don't have a wooden peg for the rubber band, use a 1¼" (32mm)-long piece of ¼" (6mm) dowel. Just drill a ¼" (6mm) hole instead of the ⁷⁄₃₂" (5.5mm) hole in the handle.

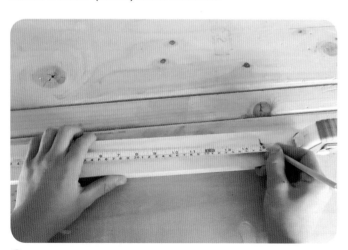

2 Measure the length of the handle. Use the ruler to measure 15" (381mm) from the end of the ¾" x 2" (19 x 51mm) board. This will be the handle. Make a small pencil mark at 15" (381mm) on the wide surface of the board. Always make your marks parallel to the lines on the ruler.

3 Mark the length of the handle. Use the square to draw a straight line across the board at your pencil mark. Make sure you keep one leg of the square pressed firmly against the side of the board. This ensures that your line is perpendicular to the edge.

Mark the saw location.

Put an X on the waste side of the line to remind yourself where to place the saw when you're cutting the handle. This trick is a good one to use in all your projects.

4 **Mark the length of the arm.** Measure and make a mark 12" (305mm) from the end of the ¾" x ¾" (19 x 19mm) board (similar to Steps 2 and 3).

5 **Secure the handle.** Mount the handle horizontally in the vise, with the end positioned outside the vise.

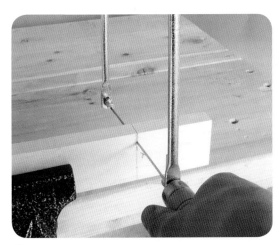

6 **Cut the handle to size.** Place the coping saw on the waste side of the line and cut off the piece of wood you do not need.

7 **Cut the arm to size.** Cut off the wood you do not need from the ¾" x ¾" (19 x 19mm) board for the arm. The round ends will be cut later.

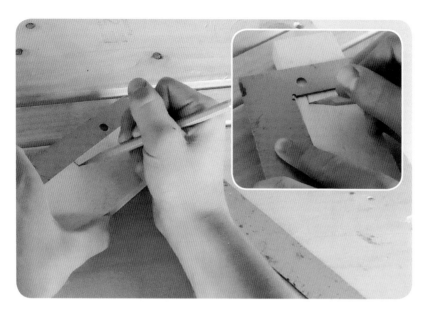

8 Mark the holes for the arm stops. Using the square, mark the locations for the ½" (13mm) holes on the handle for the arm stops. Each hole requires two measurements: one from the end and one from the side. For the first hole, measure down 2⅜" (60mm) from the end, and put a small pencil mark there. Next, move the square to the side and draw a line perpendicular to the edge through your first mark. With the square still in place, make the second mark ⅜" (10mm) in from the LEFT side. Repeat these steps for the second hole, which is 3⅝" (92mm) from end and ⅜" (10mm) in from the RIGHT side.

9 Mark the remaining hole locations. Mark the location for the ⁷⁄₃₂" (5.5mm) hole and the pivot point on the handle. Mark the locations for the pan head screw, ³⁄₁₆" (5mm) hole, and the ⁷⁄₃₂" (5.5mm) hole on the arm. Use the technique in Step 8 to mark their locations.

10 Make indentations before drilling. Use an awl to make a small indentation at the locations for the holes, pivot point, and pan head screw. The indentations will help prevent the drill bit from wandering and will get the screws started in the right locations.

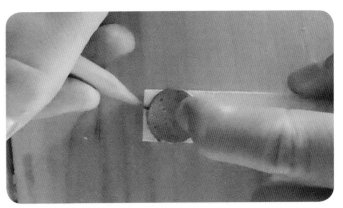

11 Drill the holes in the handle. Place the ¾" x 2" x 15" (19 x 51 x 381mm) handle on some scrap wood. Drill the ½" (13mm) holes for the stops and the 7⁄32" (5.5mm) hole for the peg (or a ¼" [6mm] hole if you are using a ¼" [6mm] dowel). Try to keep the drill perpendicular to the surface of the board.

12 Shape the ends of the arm as desired. The ends of the ¾" x ¾" x 12" (19 x 19 x 305mm) arm board can be left square or rounded. To round the corners, first mark them using a penny. Then, use a coping saw to cut the corners.

13 Drill the holes in the arm. Place the ¾" x ¾" x 12" (19 x 19 x 305mm) arm board on some scrap wood. Drill the 3⁄16" (5mm) hole for the drywall screw. Rotate the board onto its side and drill the 7⁄32" (5.5mm) hole near the end for the rubber band.

14 Measure and mark the dowel. Measure and mark a 1½" (38mm) length of ½" (13mm) dowel for one of the arm stops.

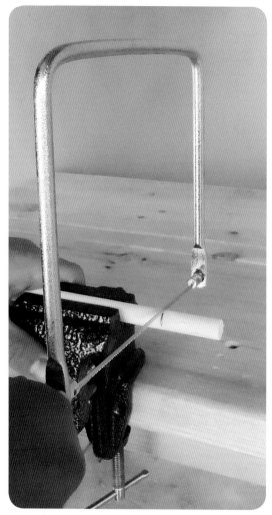

15 Cut the dowel to size. Mount the ½" (13mm) dowel horizontally in the vise with the end positioned outside the vise. Place the coping saw on the waste side of the line and cut off the piece of wood you need for the stop. Repeat Steps 14 and 15 for the second stop.

16 Insert the arm stops. Insert the arm stops into the ½" (13mm) holes in the handle so they are flush with the back. If they are loose, pound a ¾" (19mm) brad nail in from the side to hold them in place.

17 Insert the peg. Pound the peg into the ⁷⁄₃₂" (5.5mm) hole in the handle. The head of the peg should stick up about ¼" (6mm) from the top of the handle to hold the rubber band.

18 Secure the paper clip. Attach the paper clip to the end of the arm using the #6 x ½" (13mm) pan head screw and washer. Attach the narrow end of the paper clip to the arm at the location marked by the awl. The paper clip needs to be held firmly.

19 Attach the arm and handle. Connect the arm to the handle using the 1¼" (32mm) coarse-thread drywall screw at the location on the handle marked with the awl. Make sure the paper clip is on the top when you position the arm. Do not tighten the screw all the way because the arm needs to rotate smoothly.

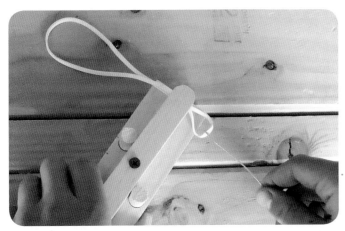

20 Attach the rubber band. Thread the rubber band through the hole in the end of the arm. Pass the loop back through itself over the top of the arm, and hook it over the peg.

21 Check your progress. With all of these steps completed, you are now ready to fling cards.

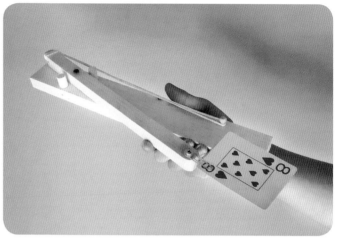

22 **Position a card.** Insert a card into the paper clip so that the paper clip is near the leading edge of the card. The long edge of the card should be parallel to the arm.

23 **Prepare to throw.** Rotate the arm back to the handle, and hold it in place with one of your fingers.

ENGINEERING ADVICE

If the card doesn't take off across the room when you release the arm, then…

- Remember, inventions don't always work right the first time.
- Try bending the paper clip so it holds the card tighter.
- Try positioning the card differently in the paper clip.
- Make sure you have enough rubber band power.

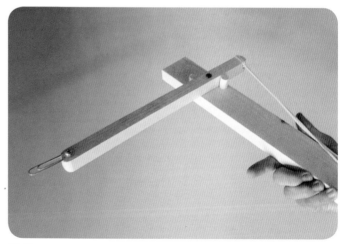

24 **Throw the card.** Release the arm by dropping your finger. The card will fly across the room at amazing speed.

Boomerang LAUNCHER

G'Day Mate! Would you like to throw a boomerang that's guaranteed not to break any windows and won't come flying back at you like an angry croc? If so, then this is the toy for you. You can make endless boomerangs out of lightweight cardboard like the back cover of a notebook—or even this book—or the plastic lid from a margarine container. Experiment with different materials and aerodynamic shapes to determine what works best. The trigger mechanism allows you to take careful aim before flinging your boomerang.

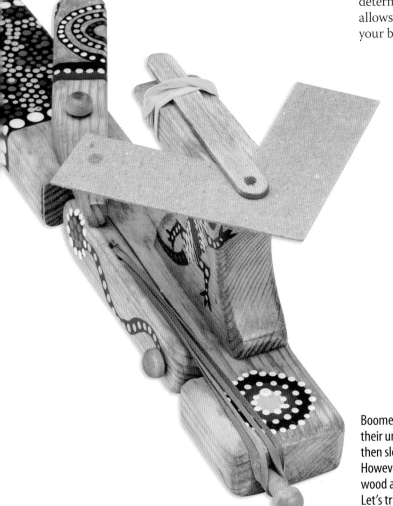

> BooMeRangs aRe pRetty exciting toys.

Boomerangs have always amazed me because of their unique flight pattern as they sail into the air and then slowly tilt in a graceful arc heading back to you. However, I'm not too keen on throwing a piece of wood and having it come flying back at me—yikes!!! Let's try inventing a smaller, softer boomerang.

MATERIALS

- ☑ ¾" x 1½" x 12" (19 x 38 x 305mm) pine board for the handle
- ☑ ¾" x 2¼" x 3¼" (19 x 57 x 83mm) pine board for the holder
- ☑ ⅜" x ¾" x 8¾" (10 x 19 x 222mm) pine board for the trigger and striker
- ☑ Three 1" (25mm) pegs
- ☑ 1½" (38mm) coarse-thread drywall screw
- ☑ Popsicle stick (Popsicle removed)
- ☑ Two #33, 3½" x ⅛" (89 x 3mm) rubber bands
- ☑ Several 3" x 3" (76 x 76mm) pieces of thick cardstock or lightweight cardboard

TOOLS

- ☑ Hand saw
- ☑ Coping saw
- ☑ Drill
- ☑ ⁵⁄₃₂" (4mm), ⁷⁄₃₂" (5.5mm), and ¼" (6mm) drill bits
- ☑ Phillips screwdriver
- ☑ Scissors
- ☑ Hammer
- ☑ Small piece of wire to pull rubber band through the holes
- ☑ Awl, or nail, to mark screw locations

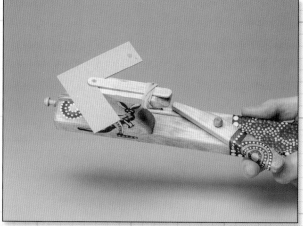

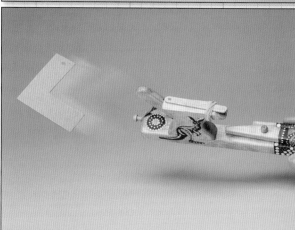

Zany Wooden Toys Reloaded!

Boomerang basics: Let's start by making a simple boomerang out of thick cardstock—like the back cover of a notebook. The boomerang is basically an "L," so let's start with that—3" (76mm) on each side and 1" (25mm) wide.

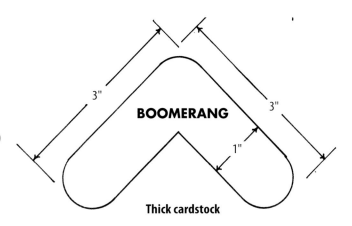

BOOMERANG

3" 3" 1"

Thick cardstock

Flinging the boomerang: I tried throwing the miniature boomerang, and it had the beautiful flight pattern of an ostrich—that is, it didn't fly. So next (there's always a "next" when you're inventing), I tried flicking it. This seemed to work pretty well, although my finger was sore after a while. I'll try to make something that flicks the boomerang.

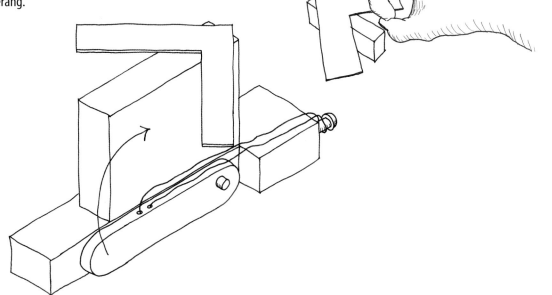

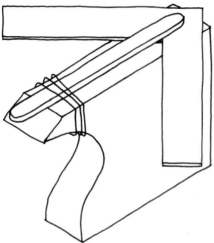

Holding the boomerang: The boomerang will not just sit on top of a block of wood to be flicked. A craft stick and rubber band will hold it in place.

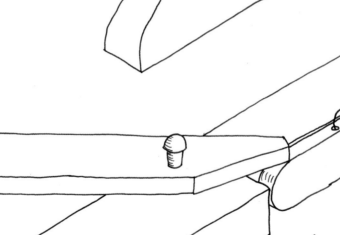

Release mechanism: The striker needs to be held down so the boomerang can be positioned correctly and then aimed. A simple piece of wood on a pivot will hold the striker down, and it can then be moved out of the way for the launch.

Boomerang Launcher

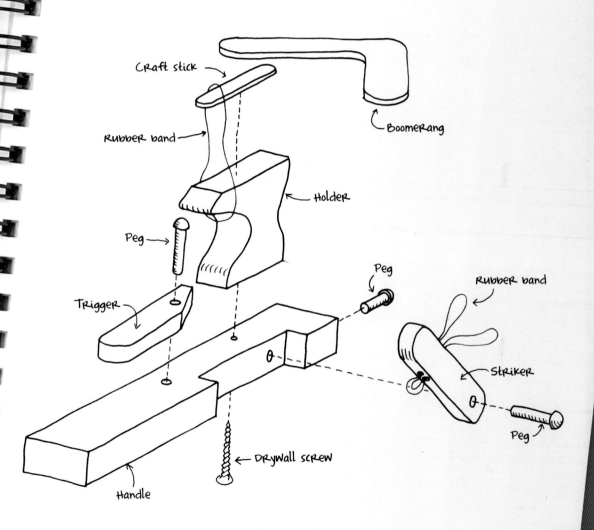

Craft stick

Boomerang

Rubber band

Holder

Peg

Trigger

Peg

Rubber band

Striker

Peg

Drywall screw

Handle

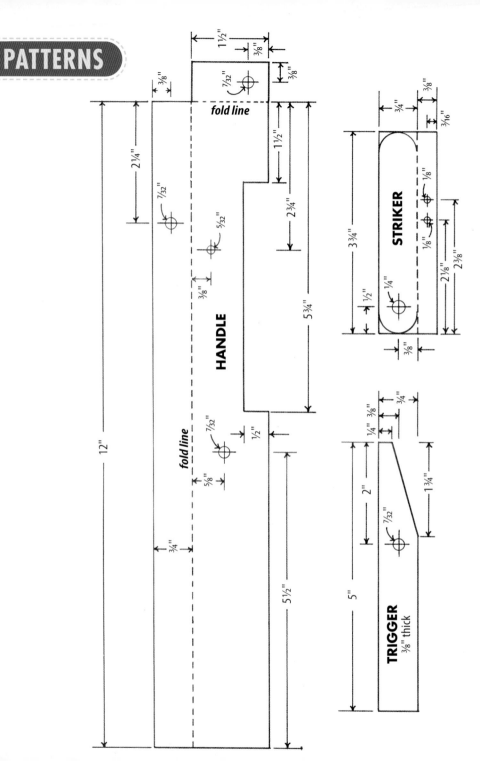

HANDLE

STRIKER

TRIGGER
3/8" thick

fold line

fold line

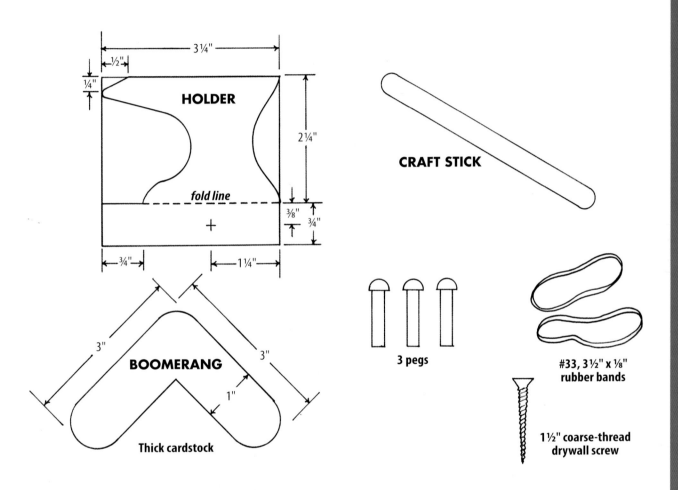

HOLDER

3¼"

½"

¼"

2¼"

fold line

+

⅜"

¾"

¾"

1¼"

BOOMERANG

3"

3"

1"

Thick cardstock

CRAFT STICK

3 pegs

#33, 3½" x ⅛" rubber bands

1½" coarse-thread drywall screw

Knobby
KNOCKER

Huh? What in the world is this? Believe me, if you build this, you'll come up with a million uses and be knocking on things all over the house and inventing all sorts of wacked-out new games. This bit of zaniness originally started out as a small, hand-held marble shooter. The first model was too short, so after each shot, the hammer would fly back and whack my knuckles. Yiiii ouch!!! That didn't rank very high on the fun scale. Prototype #2 was made very long, and that turned out to be super fun—for reasons still unknown. So trust me on this one. Just build it, and you'll have a great time.

Shooting marbles out of your hand or with your fingers is fun.

But I wanted to shoot marbles with a little more Zzzzip! I figured this could be done with a hammer that I could swing by pulling a string.

MATERIALS

- ☑ ¾" x 1½" x 45" (19 x 38 x 1143mm) pine board for the barrel, stabilizer, rotator, handle/trigger, and hinge
- ☑ ¼" (6mm) dowel, 13" (330mm) long for the rod, handle, rotator, and hinge
- ☑ Three 1" (25mm) pegs
- ☑ 1½" (38mm) coarse-thread drywall screw
- ☑ 1" (25mm)-diameter wooden ball with ¼" (6mm) hole drilled ¾" (19mm) deep
- ☑ 40" (1016mm) nylon string
- ☑ #33, 3½" x ⅛" (89 x 3mm) rubber band

TOOLS

- ☑ Hand saw
- ☑ Coping saw
- ☑ Hammer
- ☑ Drill
- ☑ ⁵⁄₃₂" (4mm), ⁷⁄₃₂" (5.5mm), ¼" (6mm), ⁵⁄₁₆" (8mm), and counter sink drill bits
- ☑ Phillips screwdriver
- ☑ Sandpaper
- ☑ Awl, or nail, to mark screw locations

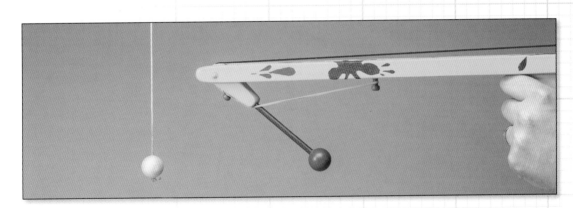

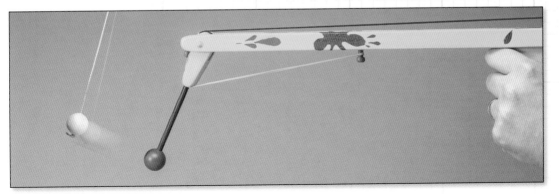

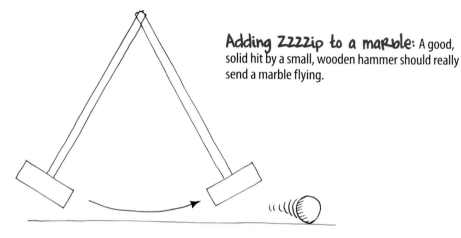

Adding ZZZZip to a marble: A good, solid hit by a small, wooden hammer should really send a marble flying.

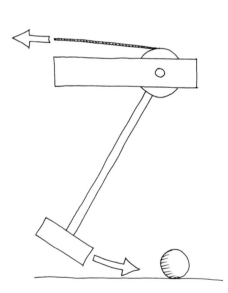

Swinging the hammer: If the hammer is on a pivot, then I can make it swing by pulling a string attached to the top of the hammer.

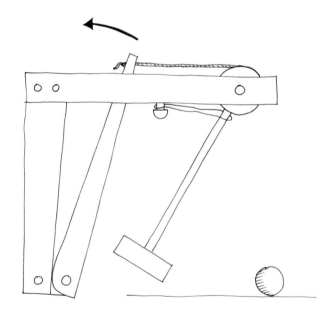

The trigger: A trigger can be added to pull the string. A rubber band will return the hammer to the starting position.

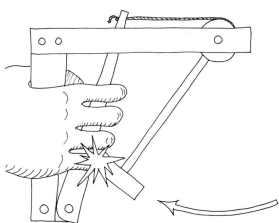

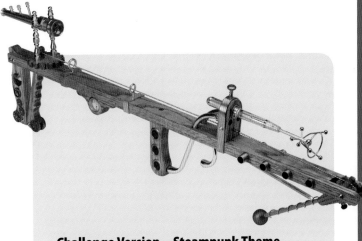

What was I thinking? Okay, this worked and really smacked the marble. However, I failed to consider that the hammer would come flying backward and the only thing to slow it down would be my fingers. Yeah, that hurt not only my fingers but my pride also.

Challenge Version—Steampunk Theme

You will have gobs of fun with a simple wooden Knobby Knocker, but if you decorate it with a Steampunk theme, it will become an irresistible attraction to anyone who sees it. You can then have more fun making up stories about its intended use. What's Steampunk? Basically, it's an art form that borrows the look of antique science and technology from the Victorian age and adds a bit of science fiction to it. Have you ever looked in the engine room of an antique steam train? It's a fascinating array of gauges, pipes, knobs, rivets, and levers. Everything was designed with a purpose, and yet that purpose is unknown to the casual observer. Now, instead of a train, call it a time machine or a plasma ray generator—and you've got the basic idea of Steampunk. So, add a few technological widgets to your knobby knocker so anyone looking at it will think there's a mysterious scientific reason for its existence that is understood only by its inventor—you.

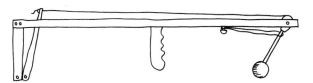

The solution: To avoid this, I made the arm very, very long and added a handle in the middle. Turns out this is a lot more fun. The hammer was also swapped out for a ball so I could hit anything.

Knobby Knocker

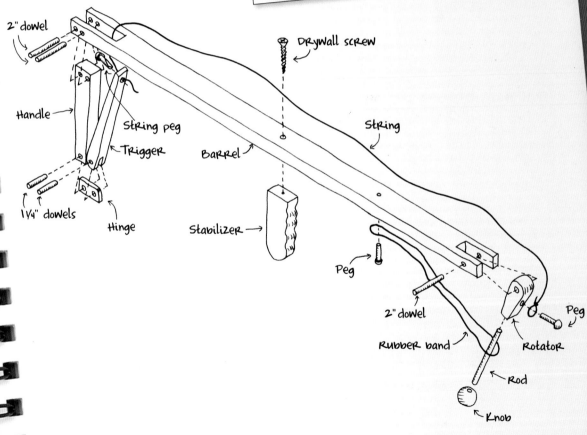

2" dowel

Drywall screw

Handle

String peg

Trigger

Barrel

String

1¼" dowels

Hinge

Stabilizer

Peg

2" dowel

Rubber band

Rotator

Peg

Rod

Knob

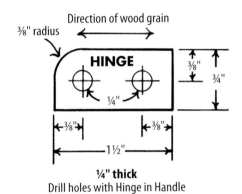

³⁄₈" radius

Direction of wood grain

HINGE

³⁄₈"

³⁄₄"

¼"

³⁄₈"   ³⁄₈"

1½"

¼" thick
Drill holes with Hinge in Handle

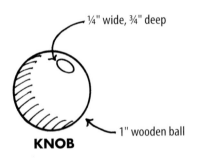

¼" wide, ¾" deep

1" wooden ball

KNOB

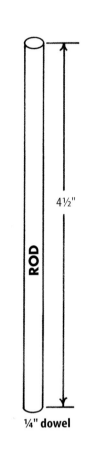

ROD

4½"

¼" dowel

2"

¼" dowel
Need 3 for Handle
and Rotator

1¼"

¼" dowel
Need 2 for Hinge

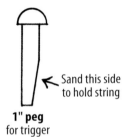

Sand this side
to hold string

1" peg
Need 2

1" peg
for trigger

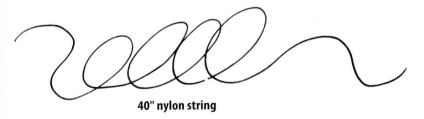

40" nylon string

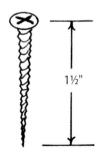

1½"

Coarse-thread drywall screw

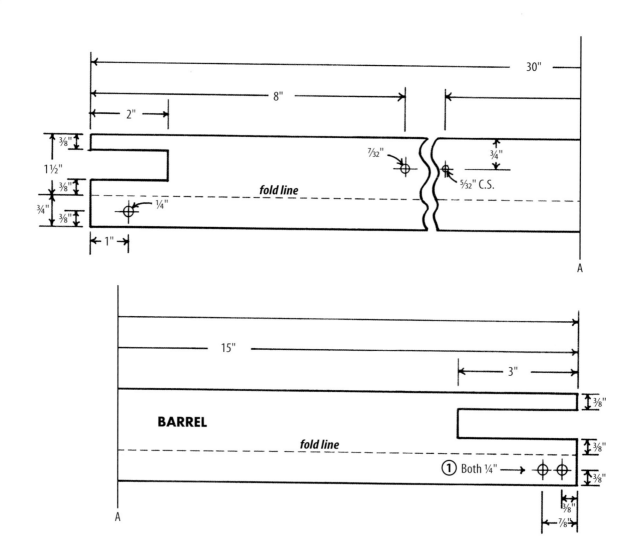

C. S. = counter sink

Note ①: Drill these holes with the Handle in place

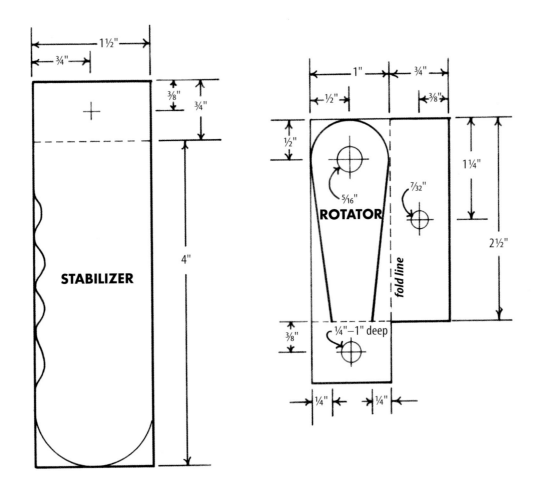

STABILIZER

ROTATOR

1½"

¾"

⅜"

¾"

4"

1"

¾"

½"

⅜"

½"

5⁄16"

7⁄32"

1¼"

2½"

fold line

¼"–1" deep

⅜"

¼"

¼"

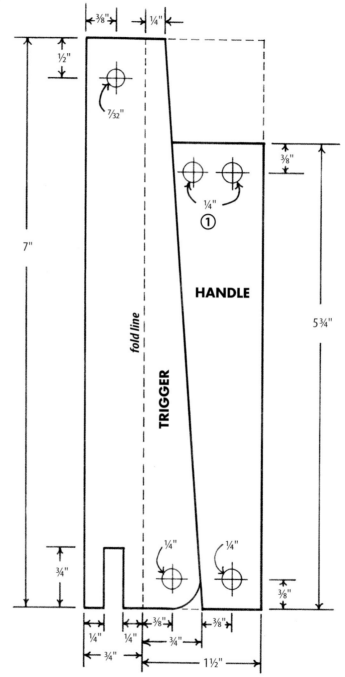

The Handle
1. Start with a ¾" x 1½" x 7" board
2. Cut groove in bottom of Handle
3. Insert Hinge and drill bottom 2 holes
4. Drill ⁷/₃₂" hole at top for string
5. Cut out Handle and Trigger
6. Assemble the hinge using 1¼"-long pieces of a ¼" dowel
7. Attach the Handle to the Barrel (see Note ① below and Helpful Hint #2 on the next page)

Note ①: Drill these holes with the Handle in place

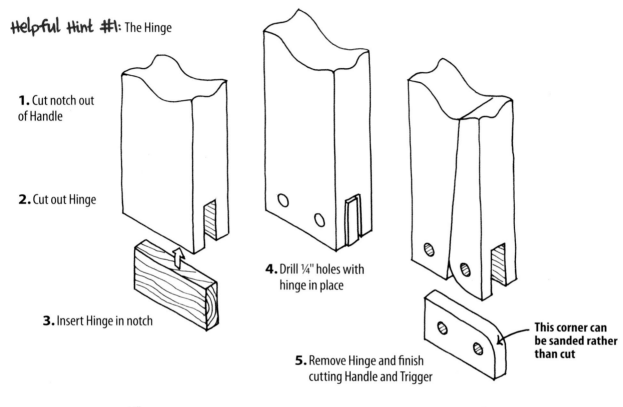

Helpful Hint #1: The Hinge

1. Cut notch out of Handle

2. Cut out Hinge

3. Insert Hinge in notch

4. Drill ¼" holes with hinge in place

5. Remove Hinge and finish cutting Handle and Trigger

This corner can be sanded rather than cut

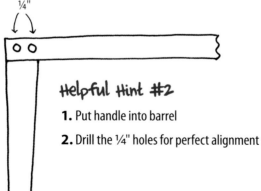

¼"

Helpful Hint #2

1. Put handle into barrel

2. Drill the ¼" holes for perfect alignment

Helpful Hint #3

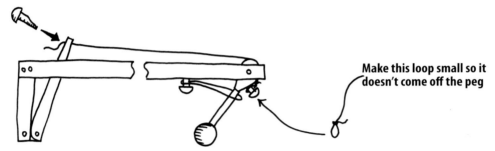

Make this loop small so it doesn't come off the peg

1. With the rubber band in place and the Trigger all the way forward, pull the string until it is taut. Hold it in place with the Peg that has been sanded down on one edge.

A Few Games to Try

Rapid-Fire Target Practice: Set up several empty aluminum cans and see how fast (and far) you can send them flying. Extra points for loud, direct hits.

Zombie Knocker: Make a zombie out of scrap wood pieces. Stack up the pieces and then try to dismantle the zombie one piece at a time.

Moving Target: Hang a 1" (25mm)-diameter wooden ball on a string from the ceiling so that it's about 6" (152mm) above your head. Make sure that the ball cannot hit anything breakable, such as lights, windows, furniture, or yourself. See how many times you can hit the ball while it's swinging.

Ping-Pong Golf: Lay a few cups on their sides around the house. Make sure they are quite far apart. Use the knobby knocker as your only club to get the ping-pong ball into the cups with the fewest strokes or in the shortest time.

Pirate
COIN MAKER

So, ye scallywags be needin' some loot for ye ol' treasure chest, aye? Well, yer 'bout 250 years too late for plunderin' and pillagin', so ye'll have to make some fer yerself. This 'ere contraption will help you turn a 6" (152mm) square bit o' aluminum foil into some fine pirate booty that would fool the likes of Davey Jones himself. But, I highly recommend ye not be double-crossin' yer pirate friends too often.

I had just finished eating a piece of Halloween chocolate and was playing with the small, aluminum wrapper.

After making it into a ball, I flattened it. I was amazed at how solid it was and how well it held its shape. So, if I could make it bigger, it would look like a coin or a medallion. It's worth a try. . .

MATERIALS

- ☑ 1½" x 3½" x 40" (38 x 89 x 1016mm) pine board for the base, sides, and compressor arm
- ☑ 1" (25mm) dowel, 2¼" (57mm) long for the coin press
- ☑ ⅜" (10mm) bolt, 7" (178mm) long
- ☑ Two ⅜" (10mm) washers
- ☑ ⅜" (10mm) nut
- ☑ Four ¼" (6mm) lag screws
- ☑ ¼" (6mm) dowel, 3" (76mm) long for the coin pusher
- ☑ Quarter
- ☑ 6" x 6" (152 x 152mm) pieces of aluminum foil

TOOLS

- ☑ Hand saw
- ☑ Drill
- ☑ ⅛" (3mm), ¼" (6mm), 5⁄16" (8mm), 7⁄16" (11mm), ½" (13mm), and 1" (25mm) drill bits
- ☑ Crescent wrench
- ☑ Dremel tool or carving tools if you want to add designs to your coins
- ☑ Awl, or nail, to mark screw locations

About the coin: Pouring molten silver is a little expensive and perhaps dangerous. Let's go for cheap and easy by using a piece of aluminum foil rolled into a ball.

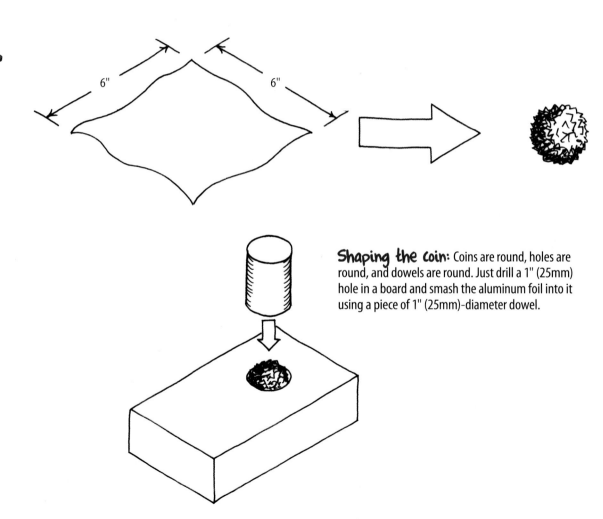

Shaping the Coin: Coins are round, holes are round, and dowels are round. Just drill a 1" (25mm) hole in a board and smash the aluminum foil into it using a piece of 1" (25mm)-diameter dowel.

Adding massive pRessuRe: To really compress the aluminum foil into a coin requires a lot of pressure. I tried stepping on the dowel, but even that wasn't quite enough. What we need is a lever to add a lot of force.

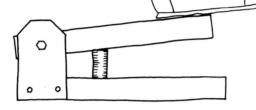

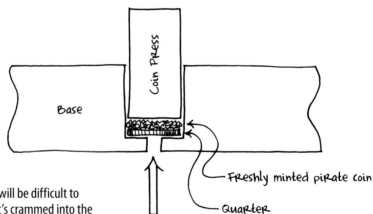

Base

Coin PRess

FReshly minted piRate coin

QuarteR

Coin PusheR

Removing the coin: It will be difficult to remove the aluminum once it's crammed into the bottom of the hole. To make it easy to remove, drill a ¼" (6mm) hole at the bottom and put a quarter in before the ball of aluminum. A small piece of ¼" (6mm) dowel can be used to poke the coin out of the hole without damaging it.

PROJECTS PIRATE COIN MAKER

Pirate Coin Maker

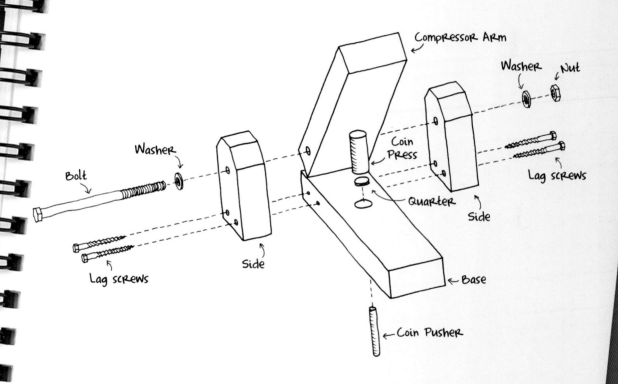

Compressor Arm

Washer Nut

Coin Press

Washer

Bolt

Lag screws

Side

Quarter

Side

Lag screws

Base

Coin Pusher

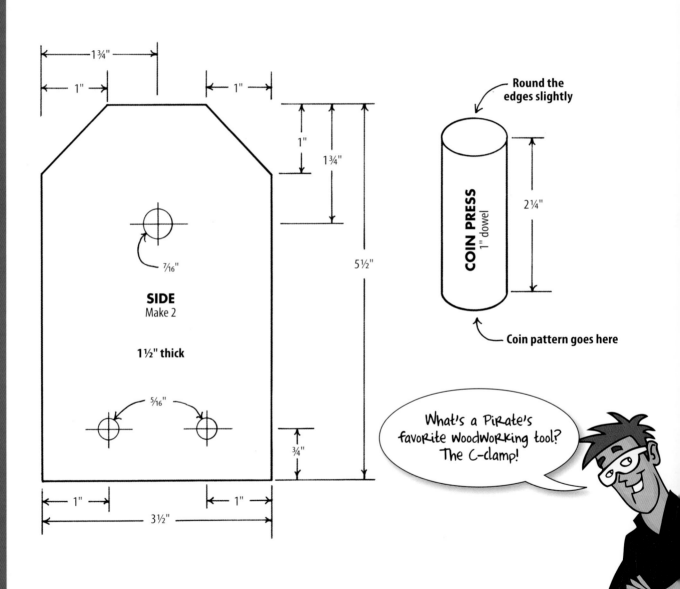

Round the edges slightly

COIN PRESS
1" dowel

2¼"

Coin pattern goes here

1¾"

1"   1"

1"

1¾"

5½"

7⁄16"

SIDE
Make 2

1½" thick

5⁄16"

¾"

1"   1"

3½"

What's a Pirate's favorite Woodworking tool? The C-clamp!

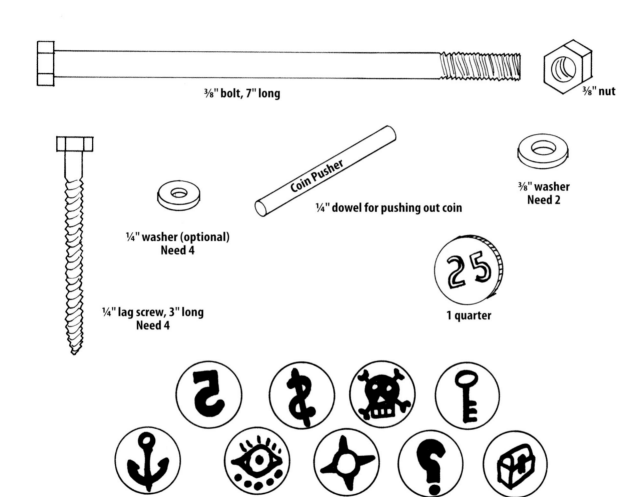

⅜" bolt, 7" long

⅜" nut

Coin Pusher

¼" dowel for pushing out coin

⅜" washer
Need 2

¼" washer (optional)
Need 4

25

1 quarter

¼" lag screw, 3" long
Need 4

Coin Designs
Use a Dremel tool to add these patterns to your coin press, or carve them.

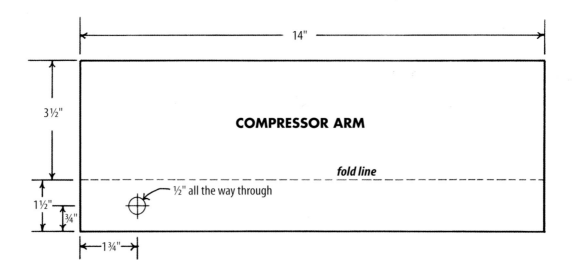

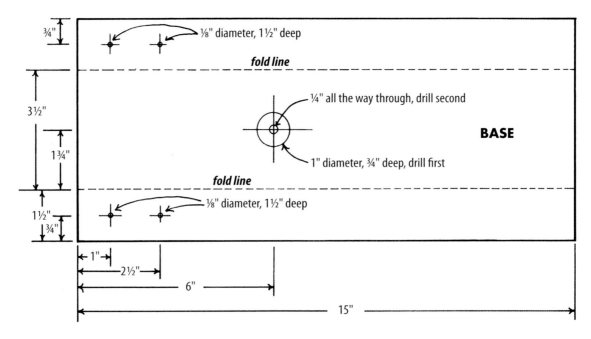

Bottle Cap
SHOOTER

What could be better than a toy that has an infinite supply of flying discs? How about a toy that has an infinite supply of flying discs—and they're all free!!! Finally, there's something to do with all the plastic bottle caps from sports drinks, two-liter soda bottles, and water bottles.

I have seen people fling bottle caps with their fingers, but I was never very good at it.

So, let's figure out the basic physics for launching a bottle cap and then build a little contraption so we can fling bottle caps all day long.

MATERIALS & TOOLS

MATERIALS

- ☑ ¾" x 5½" x 8" (19 x 140 x 203mm) pine board for the base
- ☑ ¾" x 1½" x 10" (19 x 38 x 254mm) pine board for the handle and flinger
- ☑ ¾" x ¾" x 12" (19 x 19 x 305mm) pine board for the guide and launcher
- ☑ ⅜" (10mm) dowel, 2¾" (70mm) long for the rotator
- ☑ ¼" (6mm) dowel, 4½" (114mm) long for the cap holder and launcher pivot
- ☑ 1" (25mm) peg
- ☑ ¾" (19mm) peg (1" [25mm] peg cut short)
- ☑ Two 1½" (38mm) coarse-thread drywall screws for the handle
- ☑ Two 1¼" (32mm) coarse-thread drywall screws for the guide
- ☑ #33, 3½" x ⅛" (89 x 3mm) rubber band

TOOLS

- ☑ Hand saw
- ☑ Coping saw
- ☑ Hammer
- ☑ Drill
- ☑ ⁵⁄₃₂" (4mm), ⁷⁄₃₂" (5.5mm), ¼" (6mm), ⁹⁄₃₂" (7mm), ⅜" (10mm), and counter sink drill bits
- ☑ Phillips screwdriver
- ☑ Small piece of wire to pull the rubber band through the hole
- ☑ Awl, or nail, to mark screw locations

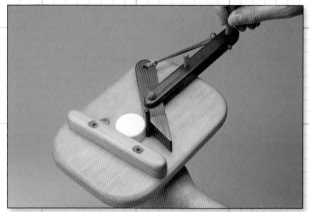

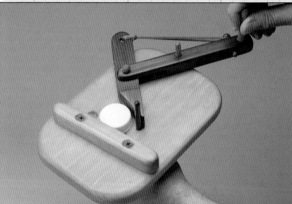

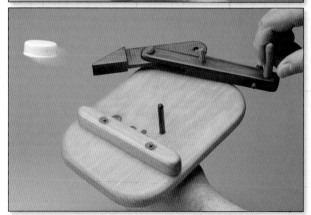

Zany Wooden Toys Reloaded!

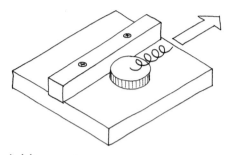

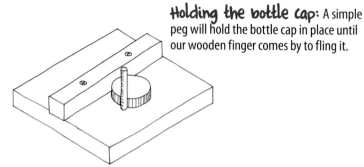

Holding the bottle cap: A simple peg will hold the bottle cap in place until our wooden finger comes by to fling it.

Adding spin: The bottle cap needs to spin through the air like a Frisbee to have a nice, stable flight. When doing this by hand, the spin comes from the bottle cap rolling along the thumb. A small board should work just as well.

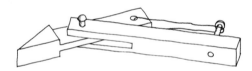

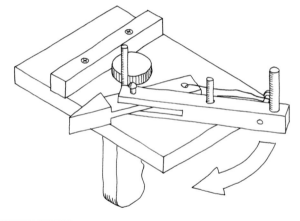

Forward motion: The bottle cap needs to be propelled forward. This is done by the index finger. Why not make our own finger using a wooden hinge and a rubber band.

Inventor's Disclaimer

There was a whole lot of trial and error in getting this to work—primarily error. For my first try I just traced my hand. That didn't work. Simple things like how much to tilt the "thumb" board took many tries. I tried adding sandpaper to help spin the bottle cap. Many holes were drilled to figure out where to mount the "finger" and where to put the peg holes for small, medium, and large bottle caps. So, continue to improve this with your own brilliant ideas and let me know when you get your bottle caps into orbit.

Flinging the bottle cap: We'll just add a handle to the finger so it can be moved forward to launch the bottle cap. The tip of the finger will bend back against the peg up to a certain point. It will then slip past the peg and send the bottle cap sailing. Let's also add a handle to the base so it's easy to hold.

Bottle Cap Shooter

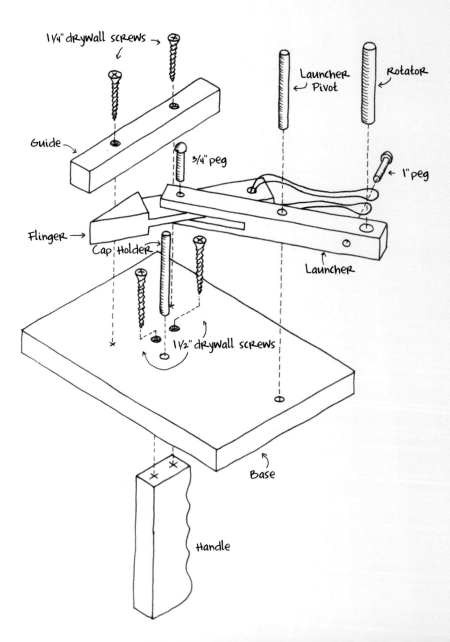

1¼" drywall screws

Guide

Launcher Pivot

Rotator

¾" peg

1" peg

Flinger

Cap Holder

Launcher

1½" drywall screws

Base

Handle

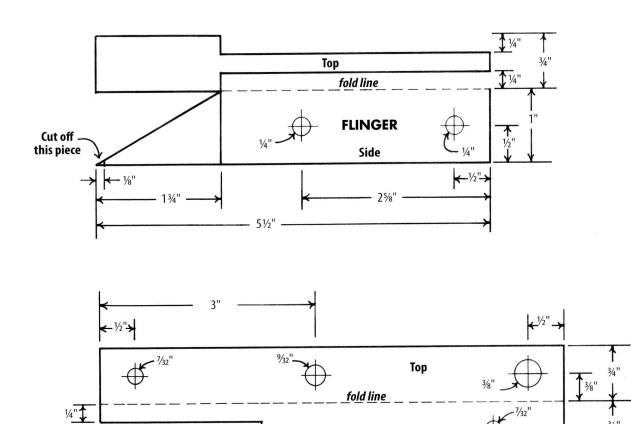

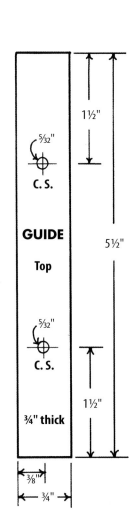

GUIDE

Top

5½"

1½"

⁵⁄₃₂" C. S.

⁵⁄₃₂" C. S.

1½"

¾" thick

⅜"

¾"

C. S. = counter sink

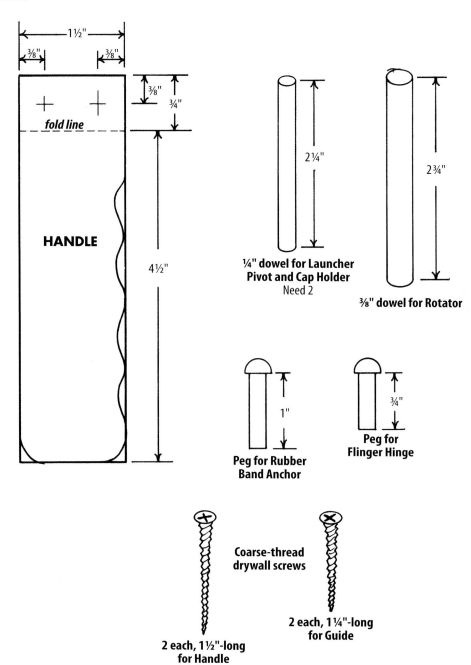

1½"

⅜" ⅜"

⅜"

¾"

fold line

HANDLE

4½"

¼" dowel for Launcher Pivot and Cap Holder
Need 2

2¼"

2¾"

⅜" dowel for Rotator

1"

Peg for Rubber Band Anchor

¾"

Peg for Flinger Hinge

Coarse-thread drywall screws

2 each, 1½"-long for Handle

2 each, 1¼"-long for Guide

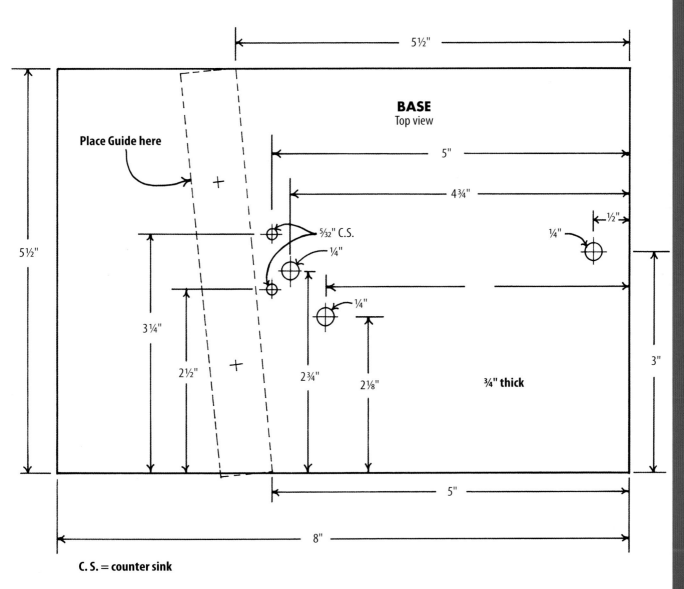

BASE
Top view

5½"

Place Guide here

5"

4¾"

½"

¼"

5/32" C.S.

¼"

¼"

5½"

3¼"

2½"

2¾"

2⅛"

¼"

¾" thick

3"

5"

8"

C. S. = counter sink

Desktop
FLICKER-ER

Have you ever been stumped trying to figure out one of your inventions? Well, after you've pondered, perplexed, and puzzled about it until there's smoke coming out your ears, then it's time to give the ol' cranium a break. That's where the Desktop Flicker-er comes in handy. Pull it out and flick some little aluminum balls around your desk, try some target practice with a pencil holder, shoot hoops into the wastebasket, or invent a new game. Meanwhile, your brain is cooling down and likely will have some fresh new ideas when you return to your problem.

There's really no purpose to this toy other than giving your brain a break.

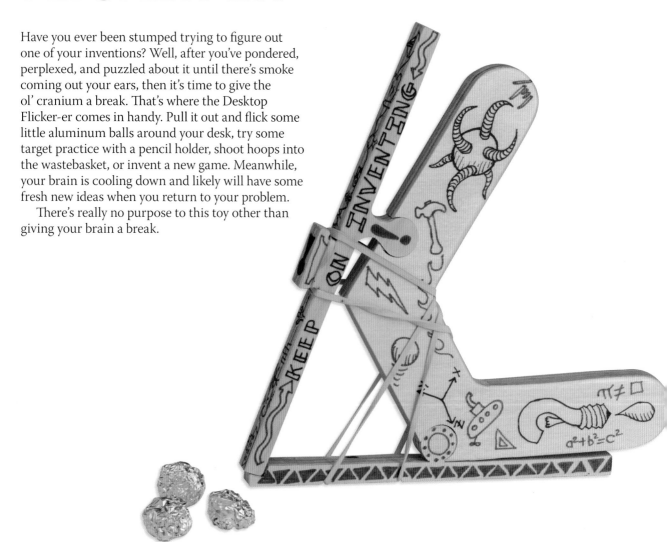

MATERIALS

☑ ⅜" x 6" x 6½" (10 x 152 x 165mm) plywood (Baltic birch works well)

☑ #33, 3½" x ⅛" (89 x 3mm) rubber band

TOOLS

☑ Coping saw

☑ Drill

☑ ½" (13mm) drill bit

☑ ⅛" (3mm) drill bit (optional) can be used for the small notches on the trigger

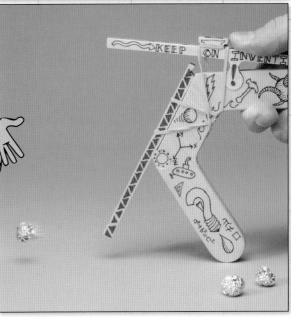

I have been on a grand quest.

I have been trying to figure out how to use the snap-action of a clothespin to either flick, shoot, or launch a small ball. I have tried, and I have failed. However, this toy was invented in the process.

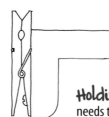

TOY INVENTOR'S WORKSHOP

Holding the clothespin: The clothespin needs to be mounted on a handle. The handle needs to hold the clothespin slightly above the floor.

Snap action shooter: The spring on a clothespin is fairly strong. If you completely open it and quickly release it, the clothespin snaps shut. That snap-action should be able to launch a ball.

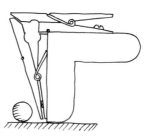

The latch: We need a way to hold the jaws of the clothespin open and then quickly release it so it can snap shut. How about using another clothespin? This works but it had to be cut to just the right length and connected at just the right distance from the end of the handle. This was a little difficult.

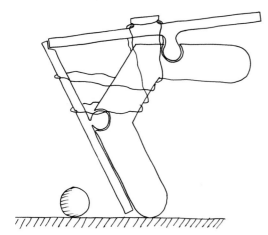

Who needs a clothespin? The main benefits of a clothespin are the pivot point and the spring. It's easy to make a pivot point out of wood and the spring can be replaced by a rubber band. How about something like this? It's the same idea with no clothespin. It's easier to make, can be made bigger, and can be made more powerful!

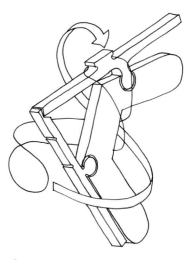

Helpful hint: Stringing the rubber band.

Desktop Flicker-er

Trigger

Handle

Flicker-er

ENGINEERING ADVICE

Just leave this toy as a blank sheet of paper. Doodle on it when you need a little extra distraction.

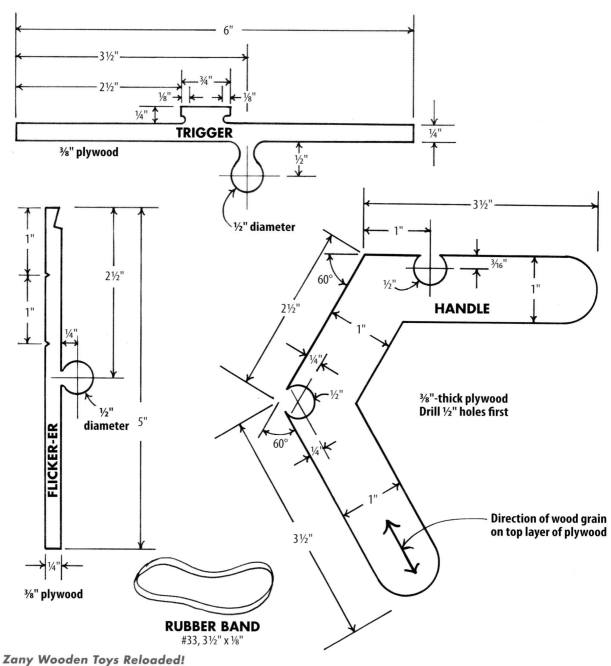

TRIGGER

⅜" plywood

6"

3½"

2½"

¾"

⅛"

⅛"

¼"

¼"

½"

½" diameter

FLICKER-ER

1"

1"

1"

2½"

¼"

½" diameter

5"

¼"

⅜" plywood

HANDLE

3½"

1"

½"

³⁄₁₆"

1"

60°

2½"

1"

¼"

½"

60°

¼"

1"

3½"

⅜"-thick plywood
Drill ½" holes first

**Direction of wood grain
on top layer of plywood**

RUBBER BAND
#33, 3½" x ⅛"

Energy Orb
ROBOT BATTLE

Our invention laboratory has recently come under attack by spy robots trying to find the secrets to our latest toys. Your mission is to invent, build, and control a robot to disarm these spy robots. As you know, the only way to defeat these spy robots is to remove the energy orb that powers them. Each orb is a sphere of highly concentrated, radioactive material (gumball) that is located in their chest behind a thick, strong layer of titanium metal (piece of paper). You must pierce the titanium layer several times to remove their energy orb while at the same time protecting your own. Once the energy orb has been removed you can use it to give yourself some extra energy (eat it). Are you up for the challenge? Hurry now, time is of the essence!

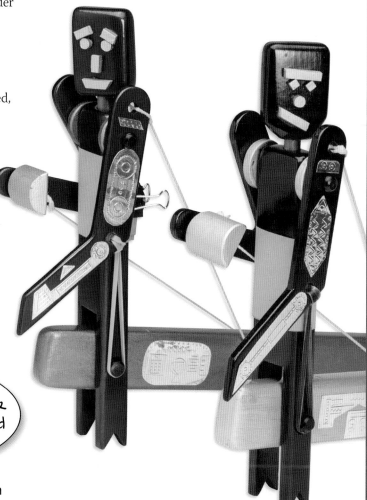

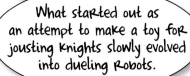

What started out as an attempt to make a toy for jousting knights slowly evolved into dueling robots.

Go figure. And what's the purpose of an epic battle if you don't win anything? That's where the gumball comes in. Now just wrap a story around your toy and you're having fun.

MATERIALS

☑ ¾" x 1½" x 44" (19 x 38 x 1118mm) pine board for the body, handle, and head

☑ ¼" x 5" x 14" (6 x 127 x 356mm) plywood for the left arm, right arm, and shoulder spacers

☑ 1" (25mm) dowel, 1¼" (32mm) long for the shields

☑ ⅜" (10mm) dowel, 8" (203mm) long for the neck and leg pivot

☑ Ten 1" (25mm) pegs

☑ Two 2" (51mm) paper clips or ¾" (19mm) binder clips

☑ 1 sheet of paper cut into 2" x 8½" (51 x 216mm) strips

☑ ⅜" (10mm) sphere of compressed radioactive material (or some gumballs)

☑ 64" (1627mm) nylon string

TOOLS

☑ Hand saw

☑ Coping saw

☑ Hammer

☑ Nuclear reactor

☑ Drill

☑ ⁷⁄₃₂" (5.5mm), ¼" (6mm), ⅜" (10mm), ⁷⁄₁₆" (11mm), and 1" (25mm) drill bits

☑ Scissors

☑ Small piece of wire to pull the rubber band and strings through the holes

☑ Awl, or nail, to mark drilling locations

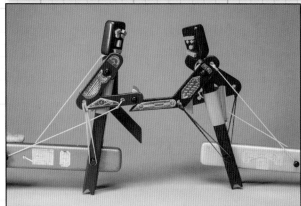

ENGINEERING ADVICE

Aluminum foil tape is a heavy aluminum foil backed with a very strong adhesive. It is available at most hardware stores, and you can use it to make awesome, metallic components for your robots. Just cut out the shape you want with scissors and then use a dull pencil to draw on gears, hydraulics, control panels, and other interesting mechanisms. Peel off the backing and stick them on your robot.

TOY INVENTOR'S WORKSHOP

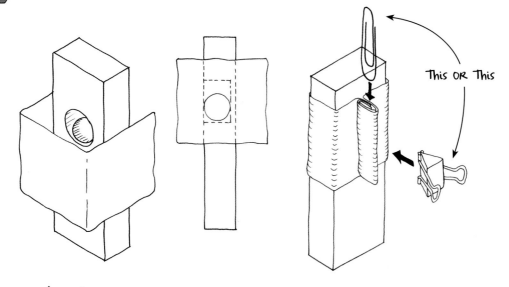

This OR This

Robot Power: Seems like this should be an orb of highly concentrated, radioactive material. Sounds dangerous. Let's use the human equivalent: Energy + Sphere = Gumball. Then, let's put it in the robot's chest and hold it in place with a piece of paper.

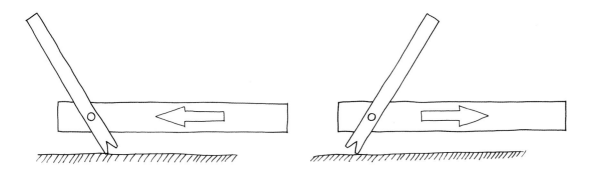

Controlling the Robot: The robot needs to lunge forward to attack and move backward for protection. We will attach a handle to our robot.

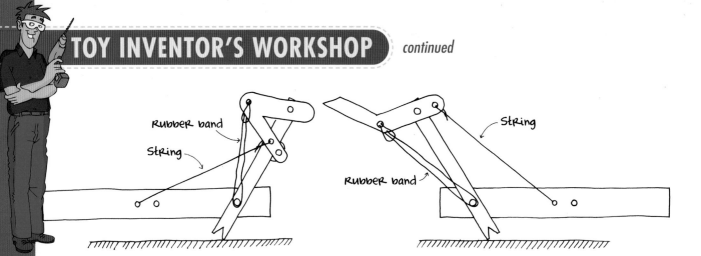

Rubber band

String

String

Rubber band

Defending: Obviously, a robot must shield his own energy orb when attacking. Use his right arm to put a shield over his own orb when he lunges forward.

Attacking: The robot must jab and rip the paper to get the energy orb. This can be done using a string to swing his left arm forward when he lunges and a rubber band to bring it back.

ENGINEERING ADVICE

1. Attach rubber bands between the arms and pivot.

2. Tie strings to the robot's arms and thread them through the holes on the handle.

3. Put the robot in the forward position.

4. Pull the left arm's string through the hole until the arm is fully forward. Hold the string in place with a sanded peg.

5. With the robot still in the forward position, pull the right arm's string through the hole until the shield is against his chest. Hold this string in place with another sanded peg.

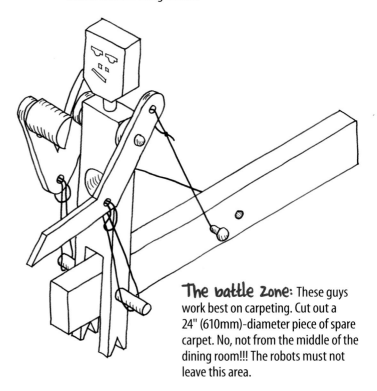

The battle zone: These guys work best on carpeting. Cut out a 24" (610mm)-diameter piece of spare carpet. No, not from the middle of the dining room!!! The robots must not leave this area.

Energy Orb Robot Battle

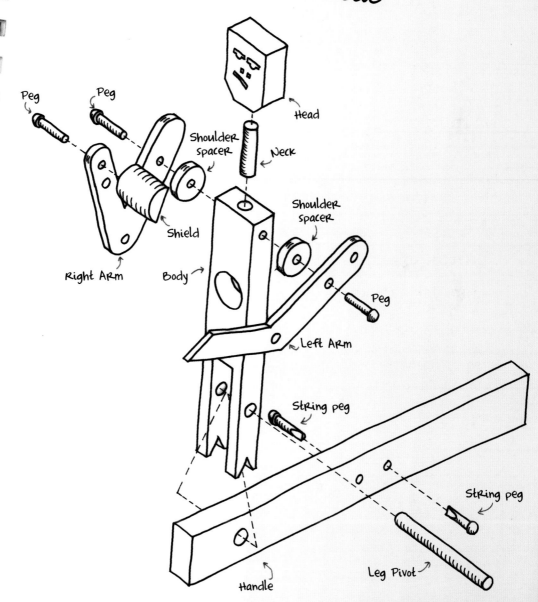

Peg

Peg

Head

Shoulder spacer

Neck

Shield

Shoulder spacer

Right Arm

Body

Peg

Left Arm

String peg

String peg

Handle

Leg Pivot

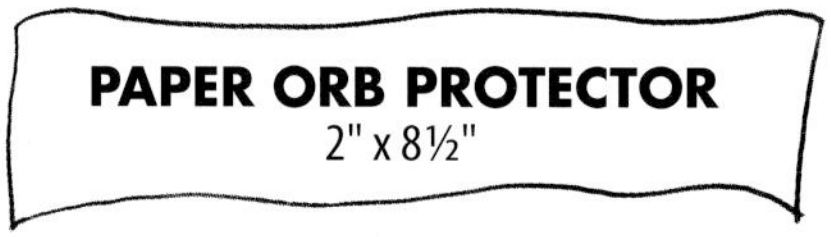
PAPER ORB PROTECTOR
2" x 8½"

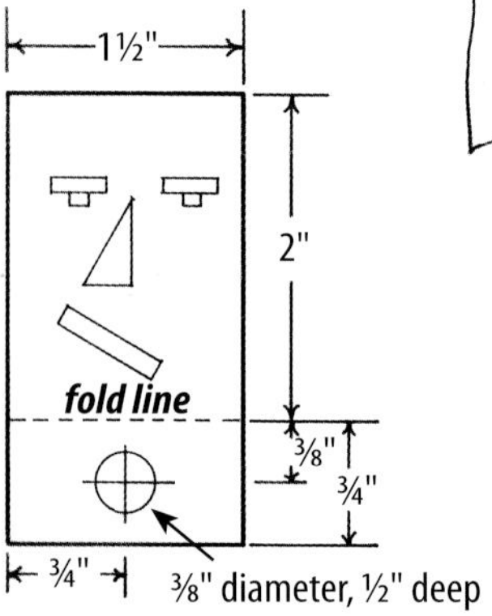
1½"
2"
fold line
⅜"
¾"
¾"
⅜" diameter, ½" deep

HEAD
Make 2

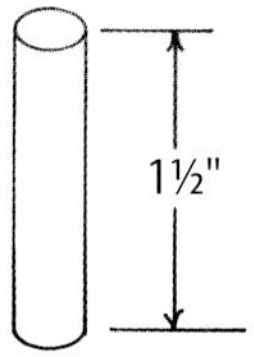
1½"

NECK
⅜" dowel
Make 2

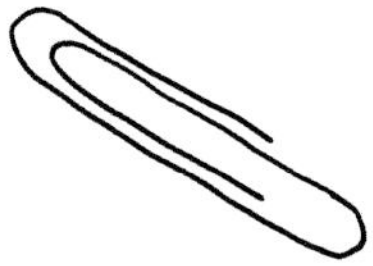

PAPER CLIPS
Need 2

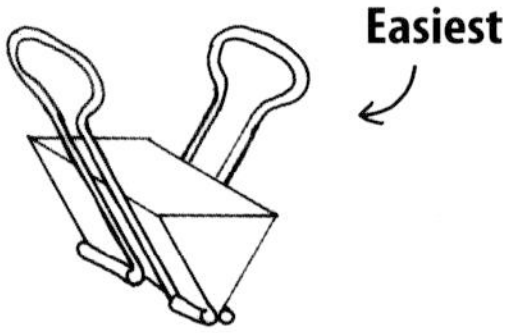
Easiest

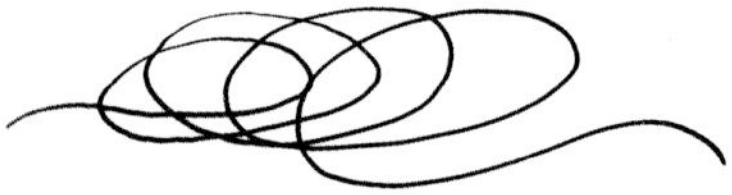

NYLON STRING
4 pieces, 16" long

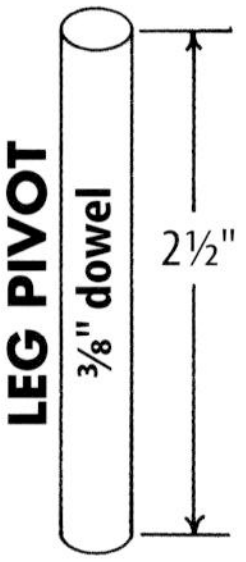
LEG PIVOT
⅜" dowel
2½"

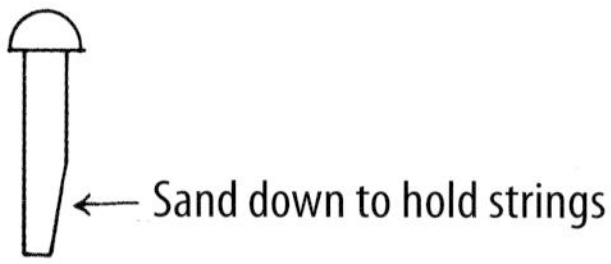
Sand down to hold strings

4 pegs for Handle

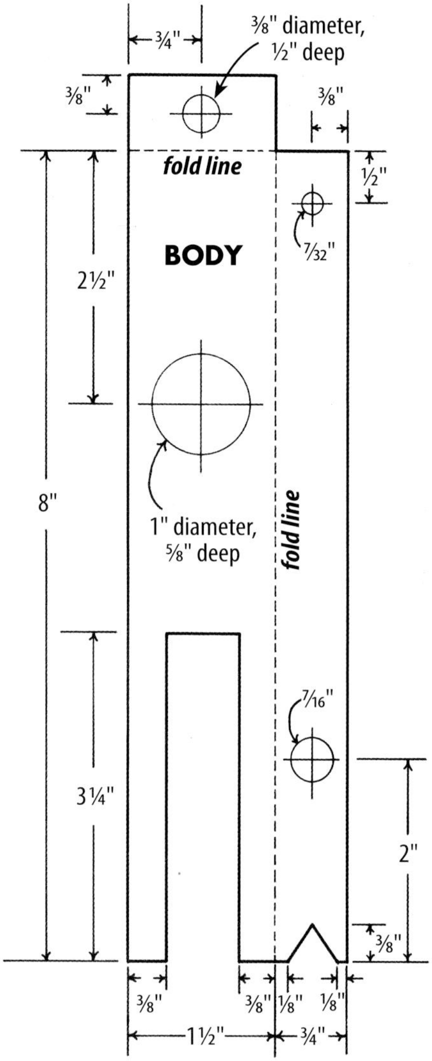
¾"
⅜" diameter,
½" deep
⅜"
⅜"
fold line
½"
BODY
7⁄32"
2½"
8"
1" diameter,
⅝" deep
fold line
7⁄16"
3¼"
2"
⅜"
⅜"
⅜"
⅛"
⅛"
1½"
¾"

Make 2

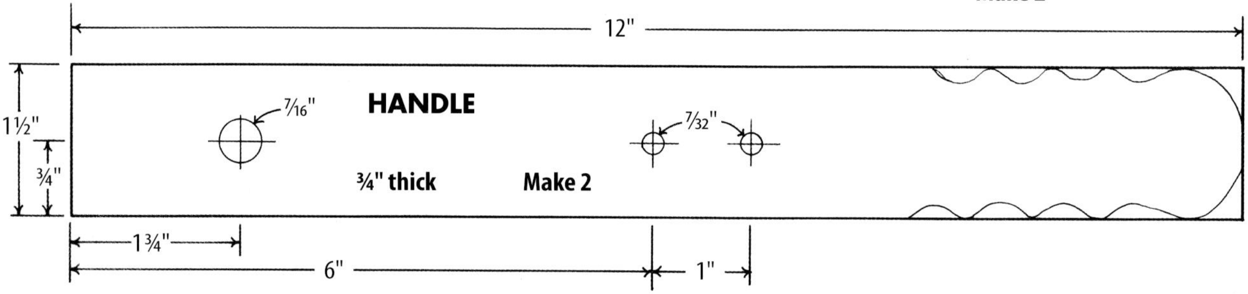
12"
1½"
¾"
7⁄16"
HANDLE
7⁄32"
¾" thick
Make 2
1¾"
6"
1"

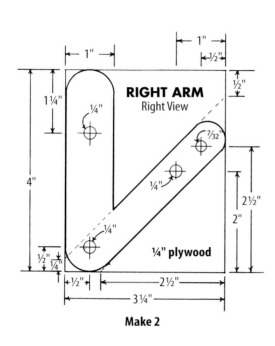

RIGHT ARM
Right View

1"

1"

½"

½"

1¼"

¼"

7/32"

¼"

4"

2½"

2"

¼"

½"

¼"

½"

2½"

3¼"

¼" plywood

Make 2

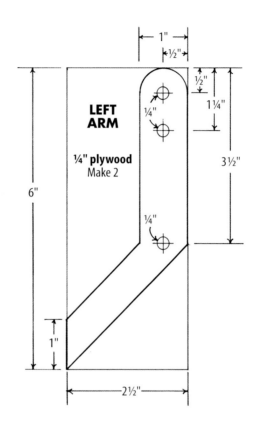

LEFT ARM

¼"

1"

½"

½"

1¼"

¼" plywood
Make 2

6"

3½"

¼"

1"

2½"

SHOULDER SPACER

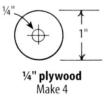

¼"

1"

¼" plywood
Make 4

1" PEG
Need 6

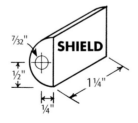

SHIELD

7/32"

½"

¼"

1¼"

1" dowel cut in half
Make 2

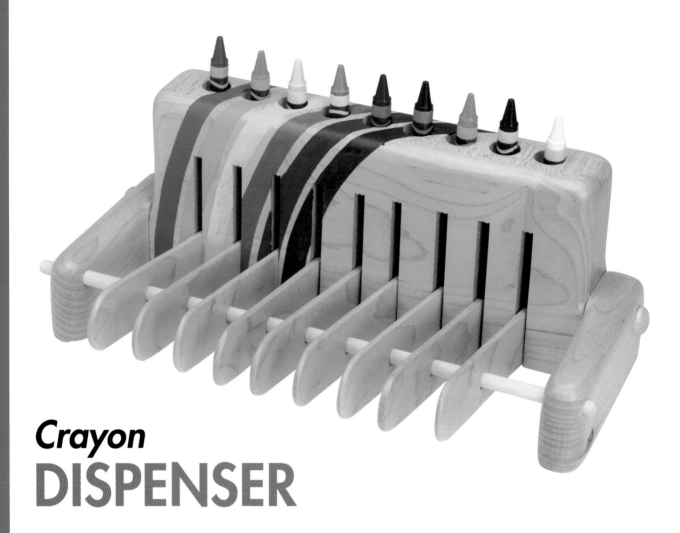

Crayon
DISPENSER

I love using crayons to add colors to drawings and projects to make them exciting and bring them to life. However, they are sometimes hard to get out of the box and hard to get back in. My first solution is to just dump them out on my desk, but then finding the right color takes time. This toy solves these problems by holding the crayons you need and delivering them when you want them. And, when you're bored you might be able to invent a game or two.

MATERIALS

- ☑ 1½" x 3½" x 8" (38 x 89 x 203mm) pine board (aka a chunk of 2x4) for the base
- ☑ ¾" x 1½" x 8" (19 x 38 x 203mm) pine board for the side pieces
- ☑ ⅛" x 1" x 48½" (3 x 25 x 1232mm) pine board for the lifters and bottom
- ☑ ¼" (6mm) dowel, 9½" (241mm) long for the pivot
- ☑ Two 1½" (38mm) coarse-thread drywall screws
- ☑ Two ¾" (19mm) wire brad nails
- ☑ 8 crayons and 1 pencil

TOOLS

- ☑ Hand saw
- ☑ Coping saw
- ☑ Hammer
- ☑ Drill
- ☑ 1/16" (1.5mm), 5/32" (4mm), ¼" (6mm), 9/32" (7mm), and ½" (13mm) drill bits
- ☑ Awl, or nail, to mark screw locations

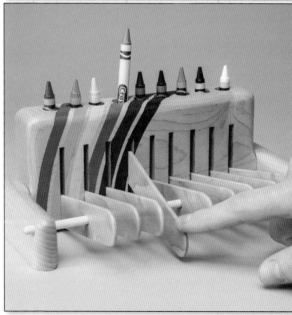

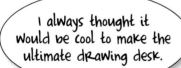

I always thought it would be cool to make the ultimate drawing desk.

When you pushed a button, a crayon would magically rise out of the table top with a hissing sound and puff of smoke. That's a little more complicated than what I really need, so let's build a crayon dispenser based on simple levers.

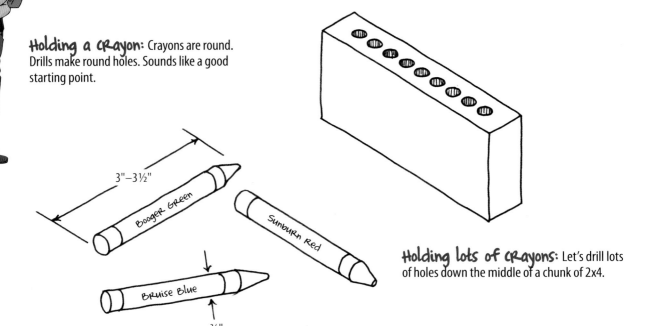

Holding a crayon: Crayons are round. Drills make round holes. Sounds like a good starting point.

3"–3½"

Booger Green

Sunburn Red

Bruise Blue

⅜"

Holding lots of crayons: Let's drill lots of holes down the middle of a chunk of 2x4.

Lifting the crayons: We want to push a button down and have the crayon go up. This sounds just like a seesaw or teeter totter. Inventors call this a lever.

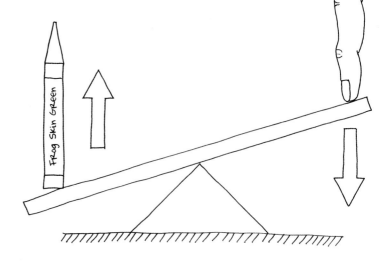

Frog Skin Green

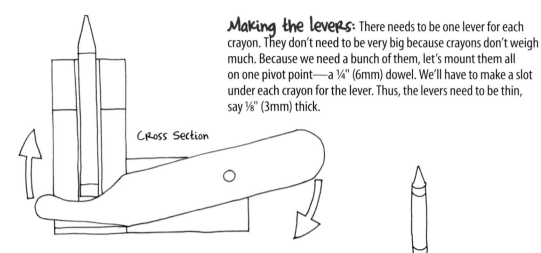

Making the levers: There needs to be one lever for each crayon. They don't need to be very big because crayons don't weigh much. Because we need a bunch of them, let's mount them all on one pivot point—a ¼" (6mm) dowel. We'll have to make a slot under each crayon for the lever. Thus, the levers need to be thin, say ⅛" (3mm) thick.

Cross Section

Notes: A nice gentle push on the lever will smoothly raise the crayon. But, a quick push will launch the crayon into the air so you can catch it and keep drawing. Way more fun. Just be careful that there's nothing directly over the crayon—especially you. Hmmmm. . .sounds like a game in there somewhere. I'll leave that up to you. For now, let's just color a picture.

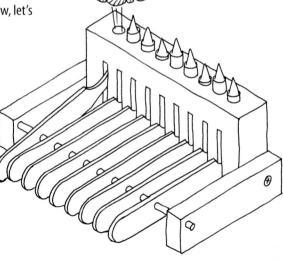

Crayon Dispenser

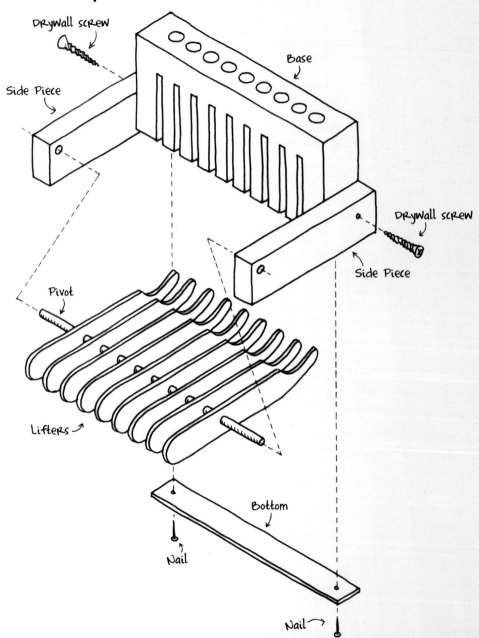

Drywall screw

Side Piece

Base

Drywall screw

Side Piece

Pivot

Lifters

Bottom

Nail

Nail

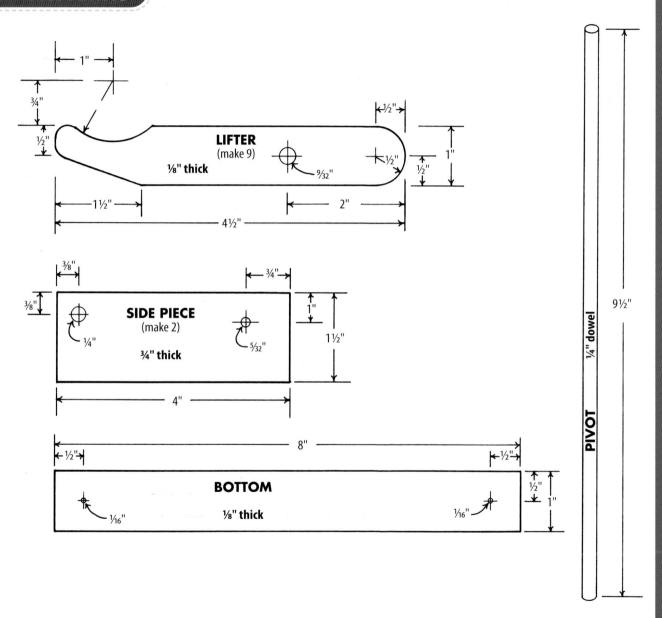

1"

¾"

½"

LIFTER
(make 9)

⅛" thick

9⁄32"

½"

½"

1"

½"

1½"

2"

4½"

⅜"

¾"

⅜"

SIDE PIECE
(make 2)

¾" thick

¼"

5⁄32"

1"

1½"

4"

8"

½"

½"

BOTTOM

⅛" thick

1⁄16"

1⁄16"

½"

1"

PIVOT

¼" dowel

9½"

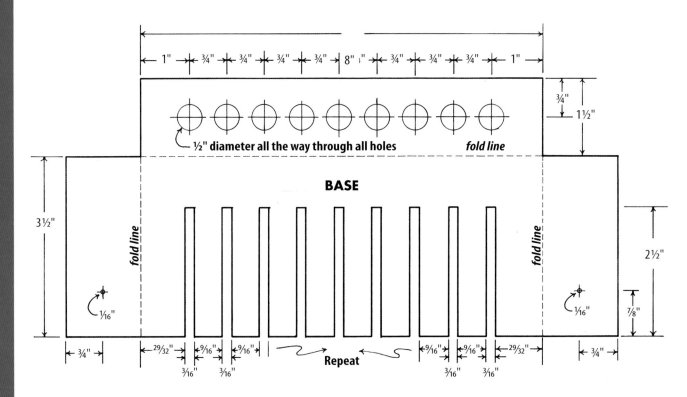

1" · ¾" · ¾" · ¾" · ¾" · 8" · ¾" · ¾" · ¾" · ¾" · 1"

¾"

1½"

½" diameter all the way through all holes   *fold line*

BASE

3½"

fold line

1/16"

2½"

fold line

1/16"

7/8"

¾"   29/32"   9/16"   9/16"   **Repeat**   9/16"   9/16"   29/32"   ¾"

3/16"   3/16"   3/16"   3/16"

ENGINEERING ADVICE

Measuring and marking all the slots for this project would be brutal. Instead, just mark the center of the holes on the front face of the base. Then center a ⅛" board on these lines and trace. OR, forget measuring altogether and just align the ⅛" board with the center of the holes in the top and bottom of the base. Trace the board to mark the slot locations.

Gumball
SMACKDOWN

Want a gumball? Just smack the plunger as hard as you can and catch the gumball on its return trip to earth. The next gumball is automatically loaded and ready to go, so keep on smacking until you've got a mouthful. Most of the fun is in the catching, so you'll have to share the extra gumballs with your friends.

I wanted a machine to shoot a gumball straight upward at the push of a button.

That's how this crazy idea started. The fun would come from trying to catch the gumball. The idea was the easy part; trying to figure it out was the challenging part. I started with pencil, paper, and a lot of head scratching.

MATERIALS

- ☑ ¾" x 5½" x 10" (19 x 140 x 254mm) pine board for the base
- ☑ ¾" x 10" x 10" (19 x 254 x 254mm) pine board for the back
- ☑ ¾" x 1½" x 21¼" (19 x 38 x 540mm) pine board for the plunger, smack pad, and pieces C, F, and H
- ☑ ¾" x ¾" x 40½" (19 x 19 x 1029mm) pine board for the flinger, and pieces A, B, D, E, G, I, and J
- ☑ ⅛" x 10" x 10" (3 x 254 x 254mm) clear acrylic sheet
- ☑ Five 1½" (38mm) coarse-thread drywall screws
- ☑ Eighteen 1¼" (32mm) coarse-thread drywall screws
- ☑ Four #4 x ⅜" (10mm) pan head screws
- ☑ Two ¾" (19mm) hook screws (I just get eye screws and bend them open to make hooks)
- ☑ #33, 3½" x ⅛" (89 x 3mm) rubber band
- ☑ Gumballs (lots and lots)

TOOLS

- ☑ Hand saw
- ☑ Coping saw
- ☑ Drill
- ☑ 1/16" (1.5mm), ⅛" (3mm), 5/32" (4mm), and ¾" (19mm) counter sink drill bits
- ☑ Phillips screwdriver
- ☑ Needle-nose pliers
- ☑ Awl
- ☑ Sandpaper

ENGINEERING ADVICE

Pegs are a toymaker's best friend. They are made out of hardwood, have very precise dimensions, are inexpensive, and can be found at most craft stores. The shaft is 15/64" (about 5.5mm) in diameter, which means the peg fits snugly in a 7/32" (5.5mm) hole (no glue needed) and a wheel with a ¼" (6mm) hole will rotate freely on the peg. The most common length is about 1" (25mm) long. I keep a handful of pegs on my workbench at all times. Pegs are used in many of the projects, however they are not required. You can come up with other clever ways to attach rubber bands, strings, and moving pieces.

TOY INVENTOR'S WORKSHOP

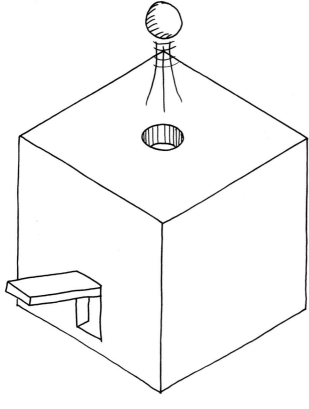

Outward appearance: My first thoughts were just about what my machine should look like. A 6" (152mm) cube with a hole right in the middle would look cool and make people wonder how it worked.

Making it Work: This is where I ran into trouble. Just drawing the basic shape, I noticed a few problems. First, there wasn't much room for gumballs because they had to be above the push button. Second, I couldn't figure out how to reload the gumballs each time. And third, I wasn't sure how high the gumballs would go with such a short lever. Back to the drawing board.

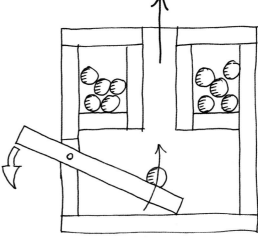

Tossing the gumball: Rather than starting with what the gumball launcher should look like, let's ask a different question: How long should the lever be to toss a gumball 3' to 5' (1 to 1.5m) into the air when someone hits it? To answer this, I built a very simple model and just tried a few things until I found one that worked.

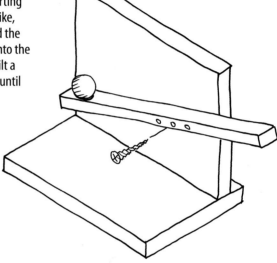

Notes

Instead of a rubber band you can also use a spring. I found a variety pack at a hardware store. The first one was too weak and didn't lift up the plunger. The second one was a little too firm, and I was worried that it would eventually pull the screw hook out of the wood. The third spring was just right. Wait, haven't I heard this story before? Wasn't there a fairy tale called "Goldilocks and the Three Inventors"? Anyway, a spring makes an interesting "sproiiiing" noise and will last longer. However, I like rubber bands because they are easy to find, and I don't mind taking things apart to fix them once in a while.

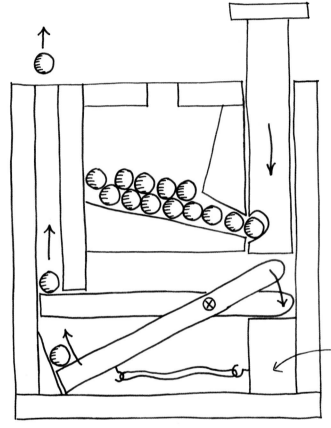

Inventor Rule #1: Keep it simple. We know what works, so let's just keep building on the model.

1. Plunger pushes lever and reloads gumball.

2. Stop for lever.

The stop will launch the gumball straight up. It will also absorb the downward force of the plunger so the pivot screw doesn't break no matter how hard you hit it.

"Stop" for Lever

Gumball Smackdown

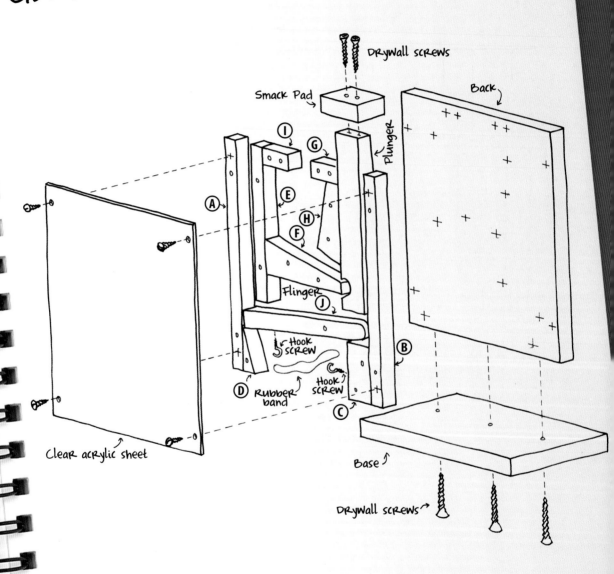

Drywall screws

Smack Pad

Plunger

Back

I

G

A

E

H

F

Flinger

J

Hook SCREW

D Rubber band

Hook SCREW

B

C

Clear acrylic sheet

Base

Drywall screws

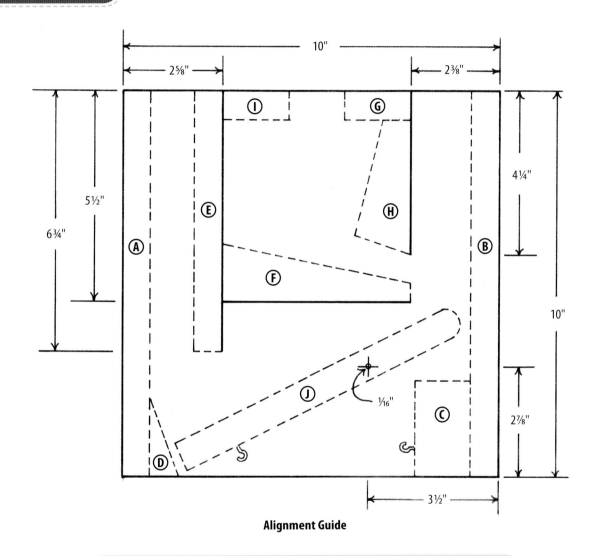

Alignment Guide

Note

Only the solid lines and the 1/16" hole need to be measured and marked.

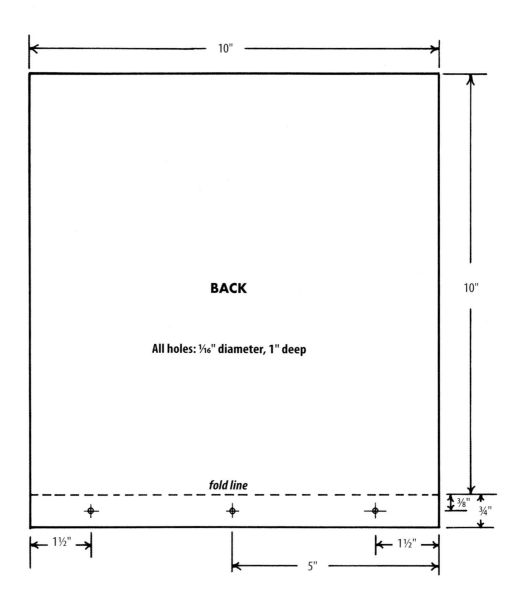

BACK

All holes: 1/16" diameter, 1" deep

fold line

10"

10"

3/8"

3/4"

1½"

1½"

5"

PROJECTS GUMBALL SMACKDOWN

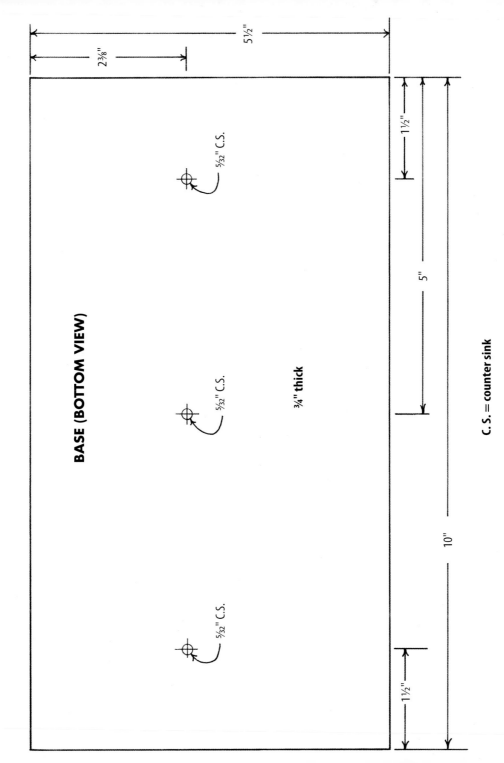

BASE (BOTTOM VIEW)

5½"

2³⁄₈"

1½"

5"

10"

1½"

5⁄₃₂" C.S.

5⁄₃₂" C.S.

5⁄₃₂" C.S.

¾" thick

C. S. = counter sink

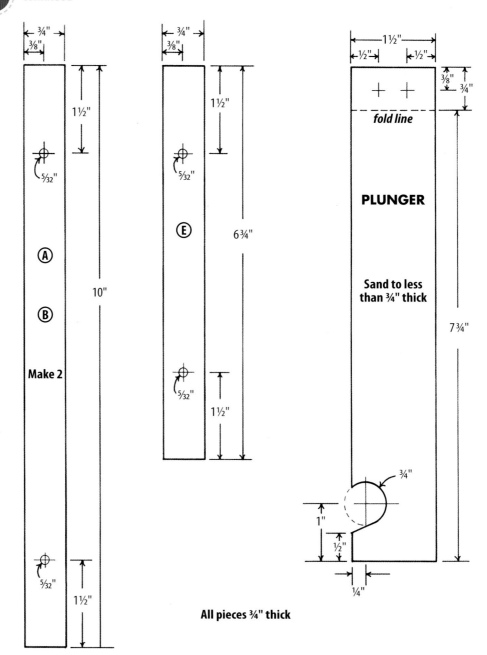

¾"

⅜"

1½"

5/32"

Ⓐ

Ⓑ

10"

Make 2

5/32"

1½"

¾"

⅜"

1½"

5/32"

Ⓔ

6¾"

5/32"

1½"

All pieces ¾" thick

1½"

½" ½"

⅜"
¾"

fold line

PLUNGER

**Sand to less
than ¾" thick**

7¾"

¾"

1"

½"

¼"

PROJECTS GUMBALL SMACKDOWN

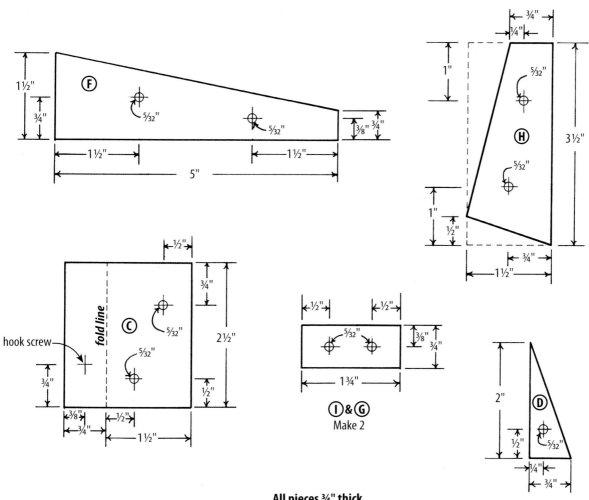

F
1½"
¾"
5/32"
5/32"
1½"
1½"
5"
3/8" ¾"

H
¾"
¼"
1"
5/32"
5/32"
3½"
1"
½"
¾"
1½"

C
½"
¾"
2½"
5/32"
5/32"
½"
fold line
hook screw
¾"
3/8"
¾"
½"
1½"

I & G
Make 2
½"
½"
5/32"
3/8"
¾"
1¾"

D
2"
½"
5/32"
¼"
¾"

**All pieces ¾" thick
Don't waste your time measuring
locations for the holes—just guess!**

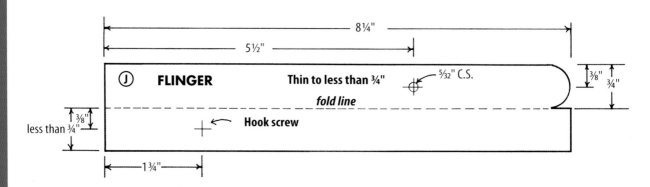

J **FLINGER**

Thin to less than ¾"

⁵⁄₃₂" C.S.

fold line

Hook screw

3/8" 3/4"

3/8" less than ¾"

8¼"

5½"

1¾"

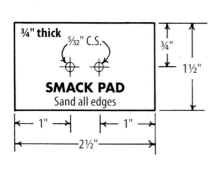

¾" thick

⁵⁄₃₂" C.S.

SMACK PAD

Sand all edges

¾"

1½"

1" 1"

2½"

C. S. = counter sink

⅛"-THICK CLEAR ACRYLIC SHEET

⅛" ⅛" ¾"

⅛" ⅛" ¾"

10"

⅜" ⅜"

10"

Index

Note: Page numbers in *italics* indicate projects.

ACQUISITION EDITOR:
Peg Couch

COVER & LAYOUT DESIGNER:
Jason Deller

COVER & TOY PHOTOGRAPHER:
Scott Kriner

DEVELOPMENTAL EDITOR:
Ayleen Stellhorn

EDITOR:
Katie Weeber

EDITORIAL ASSISTANT:
Colleen Dorsey

INDEXER:
Jay Kreider

PROOFREADER:
Lynda Jo Runkle

STEP-BY-STEP PHOTOGRAPHER:
Bob Gilsdorf

More

**Zany Wooden Toys that
Whiz, Spin, Pop, and Fly**
ISBN 978-1-56523-394-2 **$19.95**

Doc Fizzix Mousetrap Racers
ISBN 978-1-56523-359-1 **$14.95**

Natural Wooden Toys
ISBN 978-1-56523-524-3 **$19.95**

Great Book of Wooden Toys
ISBN 978-1-56523-431-4 **$19.95**

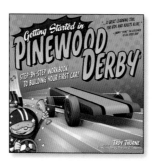

**Getting Started in
Pinewood Derby**
ISBN 978-1-56523-617-2 **$12.95**

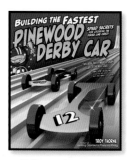

**Building the Fastest
Pinewood Derby Car**
ISBN 978-1-56523-762-9 **$14.99**

Crafty Parties for Kids
ISBN 978-1-57421-353-9 **$9.99**
DO3476

**The Art of Steampunk,
2nd Edition**
ISBN 978-1-56523-785-8 **$19.99**

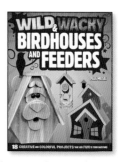

**Wild & Wacky Birdhouses
and Feeders**
ISBN 978-1-56523-679-0 **$19.95**